PRIZE POSSESSION

THE STORY OF EDEN COURT THEATRE, INVERNESS

WITH A FOREWORD BY THE LATE JIMMY LOGAN

BY JIM LOVE

ACKNOWLEDGMENTS

The author would like to express his gratitude to the management of Eden Court for inviting him to write this book and imposing no editorial control, Marketing Manager Victoria Stuart for her assistance and for compiling the index, John MacDonald, Editor of The Inverness Courier, and Tristram Woolston and his staff at Designmill Partnership Limited, Inverness, for their forbearance, Dr Jim Hunter and Bryan Beattie for peering into the future and Margaret Chrystall of the Highland News for checking the manuscript, all the people who contributed with memories and memorabilia, particularly Mrs May Marshall, Inverness, Mrs Chris Morrison, Uig, Mr Donald Matheson, Inverness, and the late Jimmy Logan who – even in the final stages of his terminal illness – bravely and generously wrote the foreword to this book. Regrettably, this great trouper's final exit came before he could play Eden Court again.

Thanks also to Rev. Derek Henderson, Custodian of the Joseph Cook Collection. Thanks are also due to Law & Dunbar-Nasmith, Edinburgh, for architectural drawings, photographs and advice, to the Herald and freelance photographers Ken MacPherson, Ian Rhind, Robert Park, Chris Robson, and to EMI, Warner and Universal Records for generously permitting their photographs to be reproduced.

Eden Court would like to thank Jim Love for his hard work in the research and writing of this book. This has been the best birthday present we could possibly have wished for.

First published in Great Britain 2001 by Eden Court, Bishop's Road, Inverness IV3 5SA

Text by Jim Love.
Jim Love hereby asserts his moral right to be identified as the author of this work in accordance with Section 77 of the Copyright, Designs and Patents Act 1988.

Text copyright © Jim Love 2001
Design copyright © Eden Court 2001

Designed by Designmill Partnership Limited 01463 229933

Printed by Nevisprint, Fort William 01397 704083

ISBN: 0-9540859-0-6

Published by Eden Court Theatre, Bishop's Road, Inverness IV3 5SA in celebration of its 25th Anniversary.

CONTENTS

CHAPTER ONE
SETTING THE SCENE   1

CHAPTER TWO
OVERTURE AND BEGINNERS PLEASE   9

CHAPTER THREE
A HOUSE OF VANITY   25

CHAPTER FOUR
MONEY, MONEY, MONEY   35

CHAPTER FIVE
"A VICTORY FOR COMMON SENSE"   45

CHAPTER SIX
CURTAIN UP!   53

CHAPTER SEVEN
ANOTHER OPENING, ANOTHER SHOW   63

CHAPTER EIGHT
CRISIS MANAGEMENT   71

CHAPTER NINE
EVERYTHING'S COMING UP ROSES   91

CHAPTER TEN
THE NEXT 25 YEARS...AND BEYOND   115

INDEX   127

EDEN
COURT

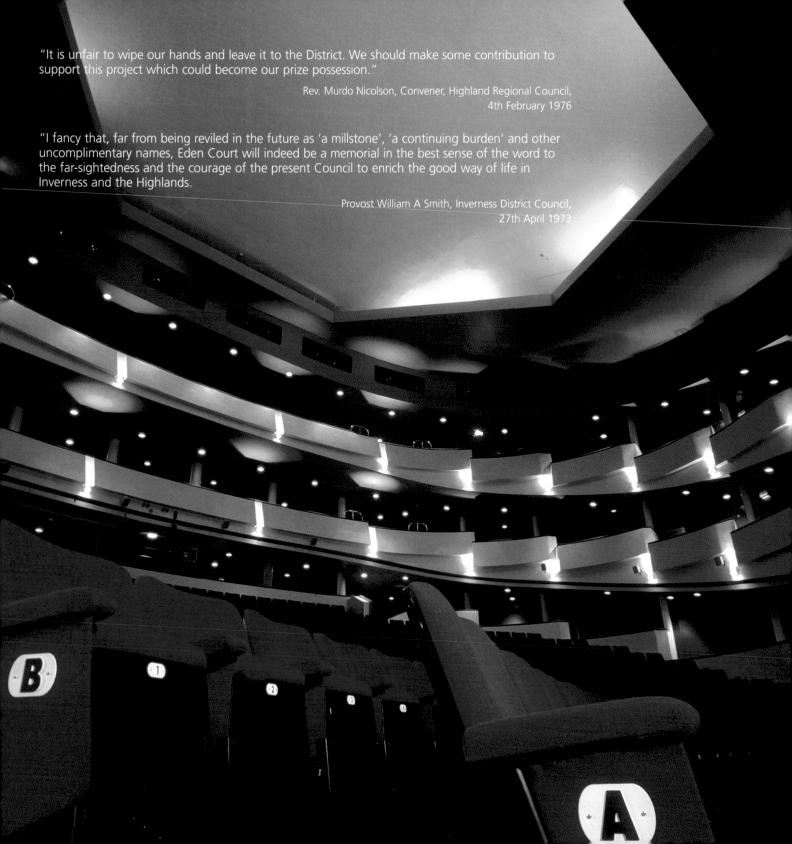

"It is unfair to wipe our hands and leave it to the District. We should make some contribution to support this project which could become our prize possession."

Rev. Murdo Nicolson, Convener, Highland Regional Council,
4th February 1976

"I fancy that, far from being reviled in the future as 'a millstone', 'a continuing burden' and other uncomplimentary names, Eden Court will indeed be a memorial in the best sense of the word to the far-sightedness and the courage of the present Council to enrich the good way of life in Inverness and the Highlands.

Provost William A Smith, Inverness District Council,
27th April 1973

FOREWORD

In my life-time on stage, I have played in every kind of hall, theatre, barn and platform from the Palladium Edinburgh to the Palladium London, The Albert Hall to the Carnegie Hall, New York, and I have never played a theatre I have not fallen in love with.

It is easy to fall in love with Eden Court which is a beautiful building on the banks of the Ness. As you look out from the stage, the very design and colour of the auditorium surrounds you and you feel you can reach out and touch everyone in the audience. Most theatres are 32ft wide on stage but Eden Court is at least 40ft wide and gives the scenery, especially in pantomime, a wonderful rich look.

I hope the following pages give you some idea of the memories the theatre has left with so many people and I still hope at some time before my final exit to return north and walk on stage again to another full house.

Picture a hole in the ground and someone saying: "They were going to build a theatre but it never got off the ground." Without Eden Court Theatre, Inverness and the Highlands would be a poorer place.

Jimmy Logan OBE
(1928 - 2001)

CHAPTER ONE

SETTING THE SCENE

The safety curtain rose stiffly, dropped and then rose again – and the well-known Scots actor Russell Hunter emerged dramatically from a Scotch mist of dry ice. Clad in Highland evening dress, he delivered a prologue written by the distinguished stage director Toby Robertson of the Prospect Theatre Company, and then paused "to deliver a wee bit o' my ain", concluding "Tak' it tae yer herts."

After nine years of inspiration and inflation, optimism and opposition, wrangling and recrimination, Eden Court Theatre, Inverness, had finally become a reality and no-one who was in the coral-pink furnished auditorium that April evening in 1976 will ever forget the sense of anticipation and buzz of excitement as the lights dimmed for the very first time before a paying public.

Off-stage 'Cassandras' were already predicting that it wouldn't last, that closure was imminent and inevitable, but a theatre that had been created against all the odds was to overcome every crisis and endure to provide many more exciting evenings for its Highland audience over the next 25 years.

Sadly, the two men who had played leading parts in the creation of Eden Court did not live to see it open – but today the late Provost William Smith's words, as emotive as any ever uttered on the stage of the theatre he and his Inverness Town Council colleague, Councillor Rev. Douglas Baxter, strove so tenaciously to build, have come triumphantly true.

Stung by opponents who branded the Eden Court project, launched by the Council as far back as 1967, as "Smith's Folly", he wrote to the Inverness Courier on 27th April 1973: "I fancy that, far from being reviled as a 'millstone', 'continuing burden' and other uncomplimentary names, Eden Court will indeed be a monument, in the best sense of the word, to the far-sightedness and courage of the present Council to enrich the good way of life in Inverness and the Highlands."

Twenty-five years on, time has proved him right and Eden Court has become "our prize possession", as had been predicted by Councillor Rev. Murdo Nicolson, Convener of Highland Regional Council. On 4th March 1976, the liberal minister of the Free Presbyterian Church who had championed the cause of progress in the Highlands, urged members of the Council to assist the beleaguered District by assuming ownership of the theatre and paying the annual interest on the loan which had been used to build it.

Although no one anticipated it then, twenty years later, another local government reorganisation would merge Region and District Councils into a single unitary authority and ownership of the theatre would have passed to the new Highland Council in any event.

Hindsight is no great gift but back in 1967, when Inverness Town Council commissioned leading theatre consultant John Wyckham to undertake a study into the feasibility of building an arts complex centre in Inverness, the town was emerging from a period when the church held considerable sway on life and was very active in opposing the spread of public houses in Inverness and Sunday sport.

Opposition might have been expected from religious quarters but no-one could have predicted that progress would be dogged by delays in obtaining approval from the office of the Secretary Of State For Scotland and that the project, when it was finally given the go-ahead, would be played out against a background of spiralling oil prices, raging inflation and the worst series of national strikes in half a century which led to power cuts, a three-day week and two general elections in one year.

Above
As convener of Highland Regional Council, Rev Murdo Nicolson's progressive attitudes seemed at odds with the fundamentalist views of his Free Presbyterian Church.

Left
Timothy West of The Prospect Theatre Company narrates and the late Sir Alexander Gibson conducts "Peter & The Wolf" at the gala opening of Eden Court on Thursday 15th April 1976.

Right
The first occupant of Eden Court –
George Eden (1804 -1886), Scottish
Episcopalian Bishop of Moray Ross
& Caithness, during whose
episcopacy Inverness Cathedral and
Bishop's Palace were built in 1869.

blocks built on the banks of the Ness and the anticipated North Sea Oil boom was expected to bring further expansion to the area.

It was this spirit of optimism that encouraged the Council to take its imaginative decision. Yet it was singularly ill-equipped to cope with some of the consequences of its decision. It was rooted in a culture of privacy – Inverness County Council had never considered so much business in secret session – and lacked the communication and presentation skills required to promote such a venture. Anticipating the biggest share of any oil-related activity, only the neighbouring Ross & Cromarty Council had the foresight to employ a Press and Public Relations Officer.

That Inverness Town, later to become Inverness District, Council succeeded in its Eden Court enterprise in the face of the ensuing public and official opposition – not to mention occasional lapses into panic – is therefore all the more astonishing and a tribute to the remarkable tenacity of its champions, to the understanding and magnanimity of Highland Regional Council and the Scottish Office, to the continuous support of its two principal funders, the HIDB and the Scottish Arts Council and, at one significant point in the theatre's later history, to its support organisation, The Friends Of Eden Court.

The site chosen for the complex was an attractive one, occupied by Eden Court, the palace that had been erected some 90 years earlier beside the new St Andrew's Cathedral as the home for the Episcopal Bishop of Moray, Ross & Caithness, George Eden. The Northern Hospitals Board Of Management acquired this large Victorian house that contained a private chapel and was surrounded by a vast lawn sweeping down to the wooded banks of the Ness when a later bishop moved to accommodation less expensive to maintain. The building was used as a nurses' home and training centre and its large kitchen garden was let as allotments.

In the late 1960s, aware that the Empire Theatre was to close – it was a converted cinema with primitive facilities for performers and audience alike and could not sustain a continuity of programme – the council recognised the need for a new performance space that could also serve as a centre for the growing market in professional and trade union conferences and identified Eden Court as the ideal site. Its use by the Hospital Board was likely to be required for another ten years, the Council was told.

As befitted the largest town in the Highlands, a centre for learning and for regional road, rail and air links with a

There was also a new system of local government that united five Highland county councils into one regional authority with responsibility for finance, roads and transport, education, social work and strategic planning & development. A second tier of district authorities was set up to administer local planning, housing, waste disposal and leisure & recreation.

It took some time for the new system to bed down and local loyalties died hard in the new regional council where members strenuously fought their own corners and took some time to acquire a wider perspective and common purpose.

All that was in the future – but, nevertheless, Inverness Town Council showed uncharacteristic boldness and vision in deciding to build an arts and conference centre. The royal and ancient burgh was already growing. Many familiar and historical landmarks, including the turreted suspension bridge and the much-altered 16th century house where Mary Queen Of Scots lodged while her army laid siege to the castle occupied by a recalcitrant governor, had been demolished in the name of progress and commercial interest.

A Highlands and Islands Development Board (HIDB) was to be set up by the new Labour government in one of the office

Right
The former Bishop's Palace was acquired by the Northern Hospitals Board Of Management and used as a training centre and residential home for nurses until 1969.

thriving economy founded on commerce and administration, Inverness had a tradition of promoting the arts with regular performances of music and drama, both amateur and professional.

The town's first theatre had been built in 1805 between Inglis Street and Hamilton Street and subsequently sold for shops and warehousing some 20 years later. The Northern Meeting Rooms, built in Church Street in 1790 by the Northern Meeting Society, an organisation of the Highland great and good, was also used as a place of public entertainment until it was sold for commercial redevelopment in the 1960s.

The Music Hall in Union Street opened in 1863 and provided the venue for large-scale musical events and drama until it became the town's Methodist Church in the 1930s. It was later destroyed by fire.

The Theatre Royal in Bank Street opened in 1882 and it too was destroyed by fire on 15th March 1931 after a performance by the celebrated Scots comedian Will Fyfe of "I Belong Tae Glasgow" fame. Among the other popular performers to appear there was Inverness-born Matheson Lang. Born Alexander Matheson Lang, he was the son of a minister of the West Parish Church who appeared with the company run by celebrated actor-manager Sir Frank Benson who later gave the young Alec Guinness a break.

Lang brought many of Benson's younger players to Inverness in "The Merchant Of Venice" and his last appearance was in perhaps his most famous role "The Wandering Jew". Guinness acknowledged it was a boyhood memory of seeing a poster for that tour, bearing the legend "Positively Final Appearance", that helped provide the title for his final book of memoirs.

Above
During the 1930s, the son of the minister of the West Parish Church, Inverness, Matheson Lang acquired a nationwide reputation as an actor and frequently performed in his hometown.

"WHAT EDEN COURT COURT MEANS TO ME"

SIR JAMES GALWAY

"You come very close to the audience…and it creates a very nice intimate atmosphere."

"I always enjoy playing in Scotland and particularly Eden Court, firstly because the people backstage are always very friendly and very nice, and secondly because of the theatre itself. You come very close to the audience when you play. You have a feeling you are among them and it creates a very nice intimate atmosphere. I feel very comfortable with the acoustic. The only problem is there is nowhere to warm up backstage – because everyone can hear you – and you have to go on 'cold'."

"The Wandering Jew" was staged in what had been the Central Hall, built as the town's first cinema in 1912 and converted into The Empire Theatre after the Theatre Royal fire. It was re-opened by Sir Harry Lauder on 17th September 1931. Another great favourite with audiences at that time was Donald Dallas, a local gym teacher and amateur actor and entertainer, renowned for his performances as Dougal Cratur in "Rob Roy". Another Dallas speciality was a parody of a Gaelic psalm intoned in a broad Inverness accent, which began:

"There was a man who had two sons

And these two sons were brothers.

They learned the English in Cromwell's jail

And taught it to the others."

Noel Coward played the Empire during the war and leading Scottish entertainers like Robert Wilson, Kenneth MacKellar and Andy Stewart appeared in summer seasons during the 1950s, but by the 1960s the programme had been reduced largely to Scottish performers and wrestling.

In 1959, a Scottish Arts Council Report noted the lack of an adequate venue for the visiting Scottish National Orchestra which, like the Inverness Opera Company, subsequently moved from the Empire to the warmer and more comfortable surroundings of the Playhouse Cinema which had little backstage or dressing room accommodation.

"The Empire Theatre really was pretty primitive," recalled Donald Matheson, a member of Inverness Opera Company who later became a chairman of The Friends Of Eden Court. "The entrance to the chorus' dressing room was virtually a ship's ladder and the theatre itself was a cold drafty place. The late John Worth would run it till the end of October then shut it down for the winter and the Opera Company would go in as the first show of the year in March. The place was always like an icebox and, once we got the heating going, the condensation would run down the walls.

"John was always mean with the coke for the boiler. It was old and he maintained it would explode if it was run too high – so I would pop round to my office to phone John and keep him talking while Scott Don nipped into the boiler room and shovelled in the coke to try and get the place warmer. John used to wonder where all the coke was going.

"When we eventually decided to move to the Playhouse, I remember going to see Forbes Irons, the company secretary of Caledonian Associated Cinemas, and asking if we could have the cinema restaurant as a dressing room – which is what they did for the Scottish National Orchestra. He said

Far right
Converted from the former Central Hall Picture House after fire destroyed the Theatre Royal in Bank Street, The Empire Theatre opened in 1931 and survived until 1970 when it was demolished and the site redeveloped for shops and offices.

Right and below
Early programme covers from the Empire and Little Theatres.

EMPIRE THEATRE INVERNESS

'Phone . . . 246

MONDAY, NOVEMBER 16, 1953

The PARAGON

by Roland and Michael Pertwee

3d.

The Management reserves the right to refuse admission, and vary or omit, without previous notice, any item of th

The British Always Rise To The Occ

If the 'occasion' arises, it takes months to train
Train **now** in your spare time.
Post this coupon to :–

COUNTY OF INVERNESS ROYAL AUXILI
AIR FORCE, RAIGMORE

Please send me details of Part-time Service
the Inverness Unit of the Royal Auxiliary Air

Name (Mr/Mrs/Miss) ....

Address ....

....

THE
QUAKER
GIRL

The Inverness Light Opera Company
(Instituted 20th January, 1924)

4TH TO 9TH APRIL 1932

PROGRAMME—Price Threepence

Forthcoming Stage Attractions
At The EMPIRE Theatre

Monday, 11th December   At 8 p.m.
THE SCOTTISH ORCHESTRA
Conductor:—WARWICK BRAITHWAITE
Leader : REGINALD WHITEHOUSE

Tuesday, 12th December   And ALL WEEK
With MATINEES on WEDNESDAY and SATURDAY at 2.30.
H. M. TENNANT LTD., PRESENTS
The Famous Play of the R.A.F.
FLARE PATH
with
PHYLLIS MONKMAN   GERALD HINZE   GEOFFREY TOONE
EMRYS JONES   PHYLLIS MORRIS   HAZEL TERRY
LESLIE DWYER   KATHLEEN HARRISON   BRYAN FORBES
IVAN SAMSON   WILLIAM GILLESPIE
This Play comes to Inverness after Running 18 Months at The
APPOLLO THEATRE, LONDON, and its tour of ITALY
and the MIDDLE EAST.
BOX OFFICE NOW OPEN

Monday, 25th December For TWO WEEKS
PINK STRING AND SEALING WAX
A THRILLER.
MATINEES on CHRISTMAS DAY and NEW YEAR'S DAY,
WEDNESDAYS, 27th December and 3rd January; SATURDAYS,
30th December and 6th January, at 2.30 p.m.

HIGHLAND NEWS, LTD., INVERNESS

Left
A poster for a professional production of "Rob Roy" held in the first Theatre Royal in 1824

Below left
Mary Campbell Macgregor catches the attention of Dougal Cratur (Donald Dallas) in a scene from "Rob Roy".

LORD CHAMBERLAIN'S OFFICE,
St JAMES'S PALACE, S.W.1.

12th January 1962

Dear Madam,

"The Captain"

I am desired by the Lord Chamberlain to write to you about the above play.

I am to say the Lord Chamberlain cannot allow the dialogue contained in the attached appendix and this must either be altered or omitted altogether. In the latter case an undertaking must be given to that effect.

Should it be your intention to substitute any dialogue then the alteration must be submitted before it may be used.

Yours faithfully,

Assistant Comptroller.

Mrs. M. McIlwraith.

Above
An example of the censorship style as practised by the Lord Chamberlain up to the early 1960's.

Below
An advertisement for an Inverness Opera Company production of "Carousel" at the Playhouse Cinema.

PLAYHOUSE . INVERNESS
RODGERS and HAMMERSTEIN'S
"CAROUSEL"
Presented by INVERNESS OPERA COMPANY
15th - 19th FEBRUARY

Left
Pictured the year before his death in 1994, John Worth was manager and musical director of the Empire during the 1950s and '60s. When the theatre closed, he started his own entertainments agency and launched the long-running "Summer Showtime" in a local hotel before becoming musical director for several Eden Court pantomimes.

he couldn't close the restaurant for a week, so we had to use the RAF Association clubrooms next door.

"There wasn't enough room in the wings and the chorus had to stand outside, sometimes in the rain, while they waited to make their entrance. The principals had the privilege of using two wee rooms at the side of the stage."

A Little Theatre had been created for amateurs at the former Flora MacDonald YMCA Hall in Ardconnel Street, giving its name to a local drama company The Florians and its function was later transferred to another small venue, The Arts Centre, in Farraline Park, also used by the film society and by Inverness Music Society for chamber music recitals. It was renamed The Little Theatre until it was absorbed by the burgh library in the 1970s.

Various other ad hoc venues in the town, including the Town Hall and various churches, were also used for public entertainment, but in 1966, the prospect of a new purpose-built theatre, which the Town Council first considered in 1948, began to materialise and the plans for Eden Court, advanced the previous year, were finally put in train.

Left
A popular singing star of the 1940's and '50's, Robert Wilson topped the bill of 'The White Heather Club' which often appeared at the Empire Theatre Inverness.

CHAPTER TWO

OVERTURE AND BEGINNERS PLEASE

As part of the commercial expansion taking place in Inverness in the early 1960s, Bridge Street was being redeveloped. Among the shops and offices on the south side was to be a new burgh library and museum with the added feature of the town's first art gallery. The Northern Meeting Rooms in upper Church Street, used for dances and exhibitions, were demolished and more shops and offices were being erected on that site. The Caledonian Hotel and its ballroom had also been torn down for redevelopment and the town's young people had to travel to dance halls in Strathpeffer and Elgin. Councillor Jack Fraser proposed that the Council build a dance hall in Manse Place.

Consideration was deferred in February 1965 when plans for redeveloping Eden Court were first floated. The ebullient, bow-tied Provost W. J. "Bobo" MacKay, an Inverness Cathedral chorister and former Inverness Caledonian footballer, proposed that the town's Planning & Development Committee consider and report on the possibility of the Council building a conference hall with provision for concerts, dancing and – to meet other needs in the towns – skating and curling. Provost W. A. Smith, who was to succeed "Bobo" as Provost, identified Eden Court as the most suitable site.

Later that year, Caledonian Associated Cinemas announced that it was to close the Empire Theatre and redevelop the site as a showroom and office block. Plans were approved by the Council in July and Councillor Rev. Douglas Baxter, who had been elected unopposed to the Council in May, told the meeting, "If the theatre is going to close, something will have to be done to replace it." Treasurer Smith said the Town still had the Playhouse and La Scala, which could be used instead.

As Gaelic entertainer Calum Kennedy led an unavailing campaign to save the theatre, the first suggestion that the Council's proposed conference centre should be designed to double as a theatre was made by James Pringle, an Inverness accountant and amateur performer with The Florians and Inverness Opera Company.

In a letter to the Inverness Courier published on 23rd July, he expressed his disappointment at the Burgh Treasurer's comments and said the town's two cinemas were unsuitable for live theatre. "Only those careless of the town's future can say we do not need a theatre," he added. "The Empire at present is undoubtedly a white elephant, both inhospitable to audiences and un-economic to the owners. It does not deserve to survive.

"Theatres have been built by local authorities before this time. Let us suppose the Council's plans for a conference hall allow for a theatre to seat 500 with an extended stage as a conference platform. The theatre would of course belong to the town and be the responsibility of a full-time official. If we as a town are able to support the kind of commercial future envisaged for the Empire Theatre, we can surely support a theatre of our own. I therefore issue a challenge to Treasurer Bill Smith to prove his words were not half-hearted and to convince the town council that an Inverness theatre is needed and is a viable proposition."

In 2001, Pringle was still involved in The Florians and Inverness Opera Company. "I remember writing to the Council and asking what they envisaged because we thought the proposed conference hall might have a use as an arts venue and the letter came back saying the building would have a caretaker," he said. "We were amazed that they hadn't considered any other uses for the building beyond having someone to sweep up and lock up after everyone had left!"

Above
Former Caley footballer, cyclist and cathedral chorister, Provost William J. "Bobo" MacKay, set the civic theatre ball rolling in the 1960's.

Left
An aerial view of the Bishop's Palace, Eden Court, and its extensive grounds, the preferred site for Inverness's civic theatre/conference complex.

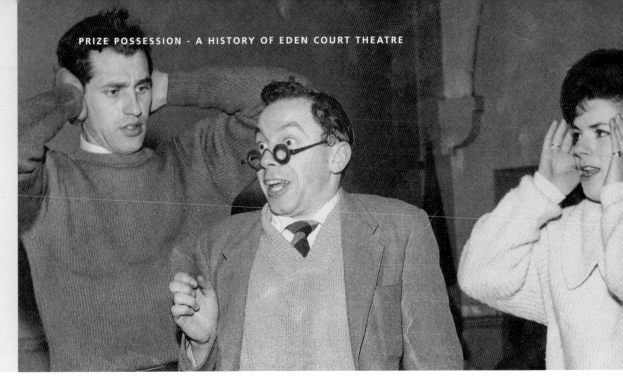

Right
Following the proposal to demolish the Empire, Jimmy Pringle, an Inverness accountant – pictured left with David Proudfoot and Dorothy MacTavish at an Inverness Opera Company rehearsal – challenged the Council to provide a replacement theatre.

Although his views were supported by letters to the Courier from the chairmen of the Highland Division and Inverness branch of the Scottish Community Drama Association, Lindsay Hamilton and James Weir, local author Mollie Hunter of The Cathedral Players and an anonymous 16-year-old correspondent, the concept was not immediately seized by the Council. It did not expect to be able to redevelop the Eden Court site for some years and continued to dither over the Manse Place dance hall.

A foretaste of what the proposed theatre at Eden Court could provide was meanwhile provided by a company called Opera For All who staged a warmly-received "La Traviata" at the Empire and the enterprising Florians who performed a modern theatre masterpiece, "Death Of A Salesman", in the Arts Centre.

Then in November, Highland Sports Club came up with a proposal for an indoor sports centre at Queen's Park which, they said, could accommodate 1000 dancers and, using acoustic roof-panels, would enhance the sound of performances by a symphony orchestra.

Councillor Baxter said the sports centre plan should proceed in tandem with the Council's plans for a conference centre and, recognising that finding a hall capable of housing the Scottish National Orchestra was a matter of urgency, the Council set up a sub-committee.

In January 1966, the Council agreed to proceed with a £100,000 indoor sports centre at Queen's Park and the following month, on the proposal of the Scottish Community Drama Association, an Inverness Arts Guild was established to co-ordinate and promote cultural activity in the town. Provost MacKay, who chaired the meeting, said he hoped the Guild would form part of Inverness's contribution to the government's national arts policy.

He invited them to form a working party and report on the need for a new theatre in the town. The group included Mr Pringle, Mollie Hunter and Jack Campbell, the head of the local Customs & Excise Office and an amateur actor.

"He said: 'Tell us what you want'," recalled Mollie who, at that time, was writing and producing for the Cathedral Players. "There was a unanimous feeling that, with the Empire going out of commission, Inverness would need a theatre. The Provost said we must consider what kind of theatre we would want, what size it should be and what facilities it should offer and, out of that meeting, a sub-committee was set up to consider these matters in more detail.

"Jimmy Pringle, being an accountant, explored the cost aspect and as I was in a position to visit other theatres like the Mermaid Theatre in London and the Yvonne Arnaud in Guildford which had only just been built at the time, I was asked to report on them and, after my experience at the Mermaid in particular, I recommended that any theatre at Eden Court should have a restaurant – and it ought to take advantage of the outlook onto the river which was a unique feature of the site.

"That and various other recommendations were incorporated into our report – but our strongest recommendation, recognising our own limitations and the fact that we were not professionals, was that, if the Council was of a mind to adopt our report and proceed with a theatre, it should appoint a professional theatre consultant. They did so and in his report to the Council, John Wyckham paid tribute to the 'valuable work' done by our committee."

Mollie, who had acted in Cathedral Players productions before taking over as producer, writing and producing the Mitford Trophy-winning play "A Love Song For My Lady" for the company in 1960, is in no doubt that the amateur companies provided the impetus for a Council-built theatre.

"They were very concerned at the prospect of losing the Empire and, although it was falling to bits, the manager John Worth had ensured that the town's theatrical tradition was maintained by a succession of professional and amateur performances," she commented. "He was very knowledgeable in terms of audiences and knew his theatre. It was sad that he had no input into the planning or running of Eden Court."

Right
An arts lover and former forces chaplain, Rev Douglas Baxter was elected to Inverness Town Council in 1965 and championed the cause for a new theatre and conference complex at Eden Court.

Right
Backing for the Pringle proposal came from Inverness author Mollie Hunter (seated right), producer of the award-winning Cathedral Players.

Above
Mollie's husband Michael McIlwraith and Dorothy McTavish in a scene from the Cathedral Players' 1960 production of Mollie's award-winning play "A Love Song For My Lady".

The working party's report was referred to the Burgh Planning Committee where the chairman, Tom Smith, a veteran Labour Councillor sympathetic to the arts and a new theatre, welcomed it. He had less than a year to serve, however and in his 1981 book, "Historic Inverness", the late Gerald Pollitt, a former member of Inverness Town Council at the relevant time, credited Councillor Baxter as "the probable originator of Eden Court and certainly its most ardent early protagonist".

"He worked untiringly, canvassing support from any organisation likely to assist in financing such a project. Once he had received a reasonable amount of such support, he raised the matter in the Council and received the enthusiastic backing of the Provost and a few members, the acquiescence of others and downright opposition from one or two."

"He had a model of Eden Court which he took round all the neighbouring councils – from Moray to Caithness – to explain and enlist their support," ex-Councillor Alistair Milne recalled. "He was clear from the very start that this would be for the cultural benefit of the whole of the Highlands, that people would travel great distances to attend events at Eden Court.

"If there were obstacles, Douglas either went over them or round them. The more the problems, the keener he seemed to get. There was absolutely no stopping him. It took nine years and he often felt frustrated but he pursued it single-mindedly to the end. When the proposal to include a studio theatre was dropped for financial reasons, he intended to ask the Gulbenkian Foundation to fund it. He was always two or three moves ahead. He and the late Peter Donald were on the same wavelength. They had the knowledge and experience to see what was required."

Councillor Baxter had firm views as to how the theatre should be, Mr Milne added. "He didn't want it to be too small but equally he didn't want it to be too big so they couldn't fill it. He wanted it to accommodate orchestras, opera and ballet but he always maintained it should cater for all tastes and for professionals and amateurs, otherwise it wouldn't have popular support and he couldn't have sold it."

"Wherever we went we looked at theatres," his widow Margaret recalled. "When we were on holiday in Greece we even went to look at a ruined amphitheatre. When you struck a match in the arena, you could hear it in the back row of seats."

Then, on 6th May 1966, the Council learned that the Hospital Board was able to bring forward its plans to build a nurses home and training centre at Raigmore Hospital and that it would vacate Eden Court within two years. The news was welcomed by the Council, which had agreed in October 1963 to acquire the property for civic developments. Councillor Baxter urged that the process should now begin as a matter of urgency.

"This is what we've been waiting for since the idea of a civic development at Eden Court was first mooted in 1948," Provost MacKay declared. "An immediate start can now be made on preparatory work for a civic centre which would be a credit to the Capital of the Highlands".

"The sky's the limit," Treasurer William Smith added. "It has to be something worthy of the town."

When the Burgh Planning Committee met on Wed 25th May, Tom Smith had retired and Councillor Baxter, the newly appointed chairman, pointed out that as the Highland Board had just submitted a report for the development of the Inner Moray Firth, the civic complex could be planned with the Board's findings and proposals in mind. He suggested the Town Hall could be sold for redevelopment, the council's offices relocated to the Bishop's Palace and a theatre/conference hall built beside it.

Referred to a special meeting of the Council, the proposal outraged the editor of the Inverness Courier and she criticised Drummond electors for returning unopposed an incomer who was now chairman of an important committee. "The Town House is in the centre of town and there is room for expansion," the leader stated. "Eden Court should be used for an arts/conference complex. Goodness knows, a decent place for drama and music is a great need."

At the special meeting in July, despite the opposition of the Provost and Councillor Baxter, the Council approved Treasurer

Right
Detail of aerial view of the Bishop's Palace, Eden Court.

Smith's motion to defer building the sports centre. Eden Court had priority, he said, and the Council couldn't do both. The editor of the Courier agreed but no letters were published for or against.

In a decision that would have considerable significance for the financing of Eden Court, the Council appointed Derek Bigg as Town Chamberlain on 25th July. An unassuming scholarly manner belied the DFC he had won with the RAF and, as an amateur clarinetist and avid concert-goer, he was the kind of incomer Eden Court was intended to attract. His assiduous actuarial skills and his quiet but unmistakable authority would prove invaluable in the battles ahead.

Councillor Baxter supported the appointment. "I remember he showed me a slip of paper he'd passed to a colleague during the interviews," Bigg recalled in 2001. "It read: 'I dig for Bigg'."

On 16th December, the Planning Committee approved the redevelopment of the northern side of Bridge Street and four days later, at its third special meeting on the subject, the Council finally agreed to extend the Town House and build an arts and conference centre at Eden Court.

Councillor Baxter's suggestion that an architectural competition for the design and construction of the complex was deferred for a month when the Planning Committee met on 11th January 1967. It was agreed that councillors should visit various recently completed civic developments to gain some idea of design and cost and Councillor Baxter undertook to discuss the project with the Scottish Arts Council (SAC) when he visited Edinburgh the following week.

The next month he reported that the SAC were willing to meet at least one-third of the cost of a civic arts centre and, while they were prepared to offer advice, they urged the Council to appoint a theatre consultant. They also suggested councillors visit civic theatres in Nottingham, Leicester, Coventry and Motherwell that were of a suitable size for Inverness.

"Inverness only has a population of around 30,000 but the catchment population is 50,000 and with the development expected between Inverness and Invergordon there is the likelihood of a considerable increase," Councillor Baxter said. Treasurer Smith congratulated him on a successful outcome.

"We must think big and we must go all out to get assistance from outside bodies," he said. "This is possibly the start of a great adventure." The committee agreed that the Chairman, Town Clerk and Burgh Architect should visit the Motherwell civic theatre.

Right
"I dig for Bigg" – Music lover Derek Bigg's appointment as Town Chamberlain in 1966 was to prove crucial to the progress of Eden Court.

Right
Treasurer, later Provost, William Smith urged the Council to defer its plans for a sports centre and give priority to Eden Court.

Above
Theatre consultant John Wyckham brought ballet and opera experience from Sadler's Wells and stage know-how from the Royal Shakespeare Company to the Eden Court project.

In its leader, the Courier claimed planners were at last doing something sensible but hoped their enthusiasm would not run away with them. "It is encouraging to those who uncomfortably and sometimes chillily form the audience in most of the halls etc. at present used for live entertainments, that something is now far more likely to be done to eradicate a very real grievance," the leader commented.

"Of course, no doubt controversy will now rage about the size and shape of the new building. What is really needed is an auditorium that, at the removal of a partition, could be expanded from 250 to 500 or even 1000 seats or else several halls of different sizes. For surely only a proportion of entertainments would command maximum audiences and the effect of rows of empty seats in a large auditorium is not only discouraging to performers and audiences but also gives a false impression of the support being given by the public, so we hope the planners' enthusiasm is not running away with them."

On 12th April, the Town's Planning Committee agreed to visit Nottingham and Coventry theatres. Burgh Architect William Jack said the Nottingham venue had a capacity of 750 and cost £375,000. Councillor Baxter reported back to the committee the following month and, on the recommendation of the Scottish Arts Council, theatre consultant John Wyckham was appointed by the Council in July 1967 to conduct a feasibility study.

A former Fleet Air Arm pilot who had gone into the theatre after recovering from polio, he became technical manager for Sadler's Wells (later English National) Opera and spent four years with the Royal Shakespeare Company before setting up as a theatre consultant and becoming involved with the redevelopment of the Byre Theatre, St Andrews.

"Considering the lack of adequate facilities in the town, I didn't find it surprising that there was a disinterest in the arts but, in the course of covering a radius of 75 miles from Inverness talking to councils and community organisations, I discovered that even outside the town, there was a pronounced demand for a theatre in Inverness staging top-class attractions." he recalled.

The intended closure of the Empire announced two years earlier, had caused widespread concern and Mr Wyckham felt sure a modern theatre of adequate size would attract major companies and wide interest. He suggested a building with a capacity of 900 seats with restaurant and ancillary facilities would cost an estimated £600,000.

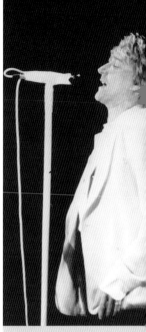

Above
As youth-orientated entertainment expanded, an unknown singer called Rod Stewart appeared with the chart-topping Jeff Beck Group at the newly opened Caledonian Hotel ballroom.

Above
Marc Bolan of T Rex, another top pop act who played Inverness in 1970.

The Planning Committee was galvanised by the report and decided to approach the Scottish Arts Council, the Highlands and Islands Development Board and neighbouring authorities for support. The Planning Chairman and the Town Clerk were instructed to seek a meeting with the Secretary Of State For Scotland; this was arranged for 19th January. Treasurer Smith described the project as almost frightening but said the Council couldn't afford not to go ahead if it wanted to justify its status as the Capital of the Highlands.

While the debate was beginning, the Empire Theatre was lying empty awaiting its first show of the year, Inverness Opera Company's production of "Rose Marie". The Florians staged "The Chalk Garden" in the Little Theatre and the distinguished pianist, Vlado Perlemuter, a pupil of Ravel, gave a recital for the Inverness Music Society. Inverness Choral Society performed Handel's "Samson" in Ness Bank Church and the Highlands and Islands Film Guild was cutting back on its services to communities without a cinema.

Provost W. J. MacKay retired in May and was succeeded by Treasurer Smith. The new Caledonian Hotel opened and attractions at the Ballroom over the coming weeks were to include chart-topping pop acts, Cat Stevens, The Move and the Jeff Beck Group featuring a comparative unknown called Rod Stewart. The rival Pavilion at Strathpeffer struck back with Millie and The Rocking Berries. Not to be outdone, The Ballerina Ballroom, Nairn, had Cream with Eric Clapton.

But government restrictions on public spending had begun to bite and the lack of progress was beginning to strain the patience of some of Eden Court's champions. At a meeting of the Council on 6th May 1969, there was an acrimonious exchange between Councillor Baxter and the Town Clerk, John R. Hill, a tall patrician figure with silver hair and a twinkle in his eye that could turn into a fierce glint.

It had been two years since the Council had submitted the Wyckham feasibility study to the Scottish Arts Council and at the previous month's meeting of the planning committee; members had expressed concern at the delay. Councillor Baxter accused the Town Clerk of failing to advise the Council of an invitation to talks between the SAC, the Scottish Office and the HIDB. Mr Hill resented the allegation and walked out.

While the consultation process ground on, Inverness did not go without its arts events. However, because of their dissatisfaction with facilities at the Empire, the Scottish National Orchestra and Inverness Opera Company switched their performances to the Playhouse Cinema. The Florians and Inverness Music Society, which staged recitals and chamber music concerts by such distinguished soloists and chamber music groups as Julian Bream and The Lindsay String Quartet – were held in the Arts Centre.

The Council changed the venue's name to The Little Theatre and entered a joint administration agreement with the newly-formed Inverness Arts Guild.

Change was in the air as 1970 was rung in. The Wheatley Commission was to report on local government reform and there were fears outside the town that Inverness would dominate a regional Council.

Inverness Town Council was obliged to raise Council House rents by 5/- (25p) and two weeks later it met the Highlands and Islands Development Board to discuss Eden Court. The chairman, Professor Sir Robert Grieve pledged support and said it would benefit the growing population of Inverness and the Highlands. Craig Phadrig Hospital was nearing completion, a new visitor centre was announced for Culloden Battlefield, British Aluminum was building a smelter at Invergordon – and the Council undertook to keep the board informed of Eden Court's progress.

Rising opera star Margaret Price and chart-topping American Country singer Hank Locklin appeared in town. The wintry weather was brightened by Inverness Opera Company's production of "Summer Song" and the bill for the second Inverness Folk Festival was announced, but the Scottish National Orchestra's concert was cancelled because of transport strikes. Local schools were hit by a national teachers' strike and the Council rejected a £200 pay rise for the Town Clerk. In the May elections, Provost Smith was returned unopposed and a General Election was held the following month.

The Florians bravely tackled "The Birthday Party" at The Little Theatre in a joint production with the Abbey School, Fort Augustus; Inverness Royal Academy staged Mozart's "Cosi Fan Tutte" with a cast that included Janis Kelly, Harry Nicoll and John Doyle, who were all to pursue professional careers on the stage. Not to be outdone, the Academy's dramatic society staged "Macbeth" and a schools orchestra was formed in Ross-shire.

At Avoch Primary School, pupils performed "Iain The Fiddler", a musical play specially written for them by composer John Bevan-Baker. The cast included his daughter Kate. Mollie Hunter was awarded the Library Association's Carnegie Medal for her children's book, "The Stronghold". "Coronation Street" actress Angela Crow starred with ex-crooner Dennis Lotis in a touring production of "Vanity Fair"

Above
Former Inverness Royal Academy pupil Harry Nicoll who, with his classmate Janis Kelly, went on to star with English National Opera at the London Coliseum, and returned to Eden Court as guest soloist with the Inverness Choral Society and to star in the 1977 Pantomime "Jack & The Beanstalk".

The Empire ends in a blaze of glory

By JIM LOVE

THE LAST night of the Empire was more fiesta than funeral, as thousands of Inverness folk said farewell to their theatre.

After 58 years of providing entertainment, the Empire's era ended on Saturday night in a spectacular bonanza of laughter, singing and dancing—but it was a finale that was charged with emotion and behind the gaiety there were a few tears.

The curtain was not rung down. Instead, during the singing of "Will Ye No Come Back Again," "We're No Awa' to Bide Awa" and "Auld Lang Syne" the curtains, scenery and props were stripped from the stage and put away forever.

FINAL BOWS

Against a backdrop of bare walls and exposed spotlights, the artists took their final bows to rapturous applause.

After it was all over performers and autograph hunters lingered about the barren stage looking rather lost. A member of the Florians Drama Group lamented: "There were almost 2500

Puma's new home

The Sutton (Surrey) puma which mauled an eight-year-old boy was taken to a new home yesterday, at Sherwood Zoo, Hucknall, Notts.

people here tonight. Where were they all when we needed them? If they'd patronised the theatre as they did tonight, we wouldn't be closing it."

The all-star line-up recaptured many of the Empire's finest moments. Compere Ron Coburn first appeared on its stage 20 years ago, with the late Johnny Victory.

HALCYON DAYS

The presence of Will Star recalled the halcyon days of the first White Heather Club and the late Robert Wilson. Bill McCue played a summer season in Inverness six years ago, shortly after he entered show business. Muir of Ord comedian Johnny Bogan first played the Empire as an amateur 15 years ago and this year turned professional. Inverness audiences were among the first to acclaim the Corries.

The Florians, Inverness Opera Company, the Calumdon Pipe Band, the Sine Nomine Singers, the Saunders MacKenzie Band and the Margaret Firth Dancers kept the local amateur flag flying, and brought the cast of the final performance up to the 100 mark.

SOUVENIR

As a souvenir of the occasion, every act on the programme received a hand-painted commemorative plaque made by Inverness craftsman Mr Hector MacDonald. An autographed programme has been sent to the museum.

The items on the programme couldn't have been more appropriate. The dancers did a routine with picks for the Empire is to be demolished

to make way for an office block. Six young mothers recalled in song their early dancing days with Miss Firth. Bill McCue sang "Bless This House," Will Starr played "The Last Post" and the Corries included some topical references in "Johnny Lad."

It was appropriate, too, that Provost William Smith and his wife were in the audience. In 1912, the building was opened as a cinema by the late Provost Birnie and his wife.

VALEDICTION

No Empire show would be possible without the backstage and front-of-house staff and the performers made sure that they were brought in on the act. Stage manager Willie Aird and his team, cashier Jean Brockie and the usherettes were all brought on stage to take a bow.

Dundee entertainer and impresario Ron Coburn provided the valediction. "A town without a theatre is a town without a heart," he said, and paid tribute to manager John Worth, who devised and produced the show, for keeping the Empire open "against all the odds," long after many other theatres in Britain had folded, and despite the lucrative offers he had received to move south.

It was fitting, therefore, that the biggest cheer of the

evening was reserved for Inverness's "Mr Theatre." He had promised that if the Empire was to go, it would go in a memorable blaze of glory and he was as good as his word.

"Be cheerful, sir; our revels now are ended."

Above
Facade of the old Empire.

Right
The press & Journal reports on the night as the sun finally set on the Empire.

Left
Alistair Gillies was among the attractions performing at the closing gala on Saturday 28th November 1970.

at the Empire and underground pop group T Rex were heading into town. The Highlands and Islands Film Guild bowed to the arrival of TV in the glens and ceased operating in August.

The regimental band of The Queen's Own Highlanders played in the 'Caley', Nepalese dancers came to town and Inverness's first Rock & Blues Festival was held at Caledonian FC's Telford Street Park. The bill, which included If, Savoy Brown, Atomic Rooster and Brinsley Schwartz, was headlined by Taste who were fronted by legendary Northern Ireland guitarist Rory Gallagher.

Despite objections from churches, the Lord's Day Observance Society and Councillor Kenneth MacLeod, the La Scala Cinema was permitted to open on a Sunday – but Councillor Baxter ensured that the performances did not begin until after evening services had finished.

Apart from wrestling, other attractions at the Empire included Calum Kennedy, Rikki Fulton and Jack Milroy as TV's "Francie & Josie" and Albion Opera's production of "The Beggar's Opera" but by this time the owners of the Empire gained permission to demolish the theatre and build an office block. Local MP Russell Johnston was told the plan could not be deferred until Eden Court was built.

Russell Hunter's one-man show, "Cocky", Andy Stewart, Alasdair Gillies and Lex McLean were among the theatre's final attractions and the closing gala on Saturday 28th November 1970 featured The Corries, Will Starr, Bill McCue and local performers.

Provost Smith, a guest at the event, praised manager John Worth for his dedication and for the pleasure he had brought to the people of Inverness. "A duty lies upon us to provide suitable facilities to maintain and encourage the arts," he added in a letter to the Courier on 1st December.

In November, Phase 1 of the town's new Raigmore Hospital had opened, Inverness County Council entertained the possibility of a bridge to Skye and major Inverness housing developments were planned at Scorguie, Balnafettack and Milton of Culcabock.

Strikes were rife throughout the country and on 3rd December the Conservative government introduced its Industrial Relations Bill in a bid to stabilise the unrest over its pay-freeze policy. Power cuts followed.

That month, in a letter to The Scotsman, two Golspie students felt Inverness was unsuitable as the site for the next Scottish university. "It offers insufficient opportunities for recreation and cultural development," they declared.

As if in response, Inverness Planning Committee began to step up its campaign for a civic theatre and started negotiating to buy Eden Court from the Hospital Board. Following a change of Government letters were sent to the Labour government's Scottish Secretary and Paymaster General seeking their backing for the project, which already had the prospect of capital funding from the Scottish Arts Council and the HIDB. If the Board was to be involved, Treasury approval would be required, the Council was told.

Provost Smith said the Council could not move until financial arrangements had been cleared and, since the closure of the Empire, the need was now urgent. "It is not a question of whether the town can afford it but whether we can afford not to go ahead with it and retain our status as the Capital of the Highlands," he declared and undertook to discuss the matter with the Scottish Secretary who would soon be making an official visit to Inverness.

In the summer of 1971, Calum Kennedy elected to use the Rose Street Hall for his touring show – and complained afterwards that it was unsuitable. Acoustics were poor and there was a lack of dressing rooms. The Council replied that the hall had not been designed or refurbished for theatrical performances.

The homeless Phoenix Drama Club that had arisen from the ashes of several amateur companies in 1966 and staged "Antigone" at the Empire, identified the empty and vandalised Bishop's Palace – now acquired by the Council from the Hospital Board for £29,000 – as a potential rehearsal space and were granted permission to use it. The Council agreed to ask its theatre consultant if the building should be retained and when he advised that it could be incorporated into the new complex, the Council appointed a caretaker.

The deadlock that had stalled the Eden Court project was finally broken on 1st November when the Council, which blamed the Scottish Office for the delay, finally heard that the Secretary Of State For Scotland, William Ross, had offered to meet Council representatives in Edinburgh on 3rd December.

At its next monthly meeting, Provost William Smith, fresh from the talks, reported that the Scottish Office had agreed to pay half the estimated cost of Eden Court which would be paid through the Highland Board and the Scottish Arts Council, provided the Council raised the remaining £300,000 – £225,000 from the rates and £75,000 by public appeal.

"I was astonished to learn that the Scottish Arts Council got only £500,000 for the whole country," Provost Smith revealed. "We would therefore be very fortunate to get £150,000. We are competing with Glasgow, Perth, Dundee and Pitlochry and it is important we get a well-planned scheme going at once, otherwise we may lose our place in the queue." Even if the money was raised sooner, it would be 1973 before building could start and he urged the council to go all out for the project because of the great benefit it would be to Inverness and the Highlands.

The Council unanimously agreed to ask its consultant to draw up a brief as a matter of urgency. The decision was welcomed next day as "good news" in the Inverness Courier's leader column. "Before anyone starts pointing out that the town needs other things before – and perhaps even more – than such a complex, let us point out that the money being offered by the government is only for the Eden Court development and no reciprocal amount from the town council will mean no grant. Therefore it behoves all those who feel strongly that such a centre is essential, not merely desirable, to see that it comes into being.

"For ourselves, we think it is a bit too ambitious. A theatre or hall to seat 500 or so is what Inverness really needs and indeed has needed for long enough. The Little Theatre, the Town Hall and those usually available being too small, the Empire Theatre and Playhouse Cinema too large for most entertainments, meetings and the like. Indeed if memory serves us right, the only occasion when the Empire was filled to capacity, at least since the end of the war, was for the Scottish finals of the drama festival and one or two orchestral concerts, world famous solo singers or pianists and one or two outstanding variety entertainers, and accommodating a smaller audience seems the first priority.

"However as we keep being warned about the vast population increase which is to live in and around Inverness

Right
Initially a supporter of Eden Court
Eveline Barron, editor and proprietor
of the Inverness Courier, became an
increasingly vociferous opponent as
the cost increased.

in the near future, perhaps the larger one would be a prudent venture. On the other hand, could there not be a compromise, such as room for expansion with enough internal fittings to vary the size of the auditorium?

"Be that as it may, the opportunity for Inverness and the Highlands to translate this good news into a solid, satisfying and satisfactory centre lies to hand. It will be sad if it is missed and surely ratepayers would not begrudge a few pence more."

Sighs of relief must have been breathed in the Town House. Inverness's most widely-read newspaper and its formidably critical and combative editor, Eveline Barron, was on-side – but it wasn't necessary to read between the lines to spot that she had her own ideas as to the form the new centre should take and how the project should develop.

At its January 1972 meeting, Councillor Baxter moved that the Council discuss the appointment of architects and, in the presence of its theatre consultant, representatives of quantity surveyors Souter & Jaffrey and Scottish Arts Council director Sandy Dunbar, it was agreed that the Edinburgh firm of Law & Dunbar-Nasmith, should be awarded the brief. "We were recommended for the job by John Wyckham with whom we were already working on proposals for the new theatre at Pitlochry, which although pre-dating Inverness in terms of commission, did not get built until Eden Court was

complete," recalled Sir James Dunbar-Nasmith who was president of the Royal Incorporation Of Architects in Scotland at that time.

At a public meeting four days later, Mr Dunbar welcomed the Council's decision and its commitment in keeping the project alive for four years, even when it seemed government support would not be forthcoming. The Scottish Arts Council was very impressed and excited by the scheme and the chosen site was magnificent, he added.

Provost Smith expressed complete confidence in the public raising the necessary £75,000. "It is by no means a parochial project," he declared. "It has always been a dream of mine, shared by the Town Council, that some day we would have a cultural centre worthy of the Highland Capital which would serve the whole Highland Region. I've received letters of support from the Black Isle, Kyle, Grantown and many other places in the Highlands." An appeal committee would be appointed, he said.

Mr Wyckham said the theatre would cater for a variety of tastes and high quality of performance. He visualised an auditorium seating 750 -1000 people and designed for any kind of performance and, more presciently than he perhaps realised at the time, he added that in order to prevent costs rising, work would have to be carried out quickly. Graham Law, Dunbar-Nasmith's partner – who, as a result of his

success with Eden Court, was to go on to design a number of important theatres elsewhere – said he hoped the Bishop's Palace could be incorporated into his design. He anticipated construction would begin in the spring of 1973 with completion in the summer of 1974.

Having briefed the Council, the design team set to work in January 1972 and would complete their brief by November when the project went out to tender. "There was an instant marriage of minds because the team shared an enthusiasm for a three-tier design in which the walls of the auditorium would be 'papered with people'," auditorium adviser Iain Mackintosh said.

Considerable research went into the design of Eden Court. "Graham and I were both very keen on theatre and opera and were determined that this would not just be a good theatre but that it would be the best of its size currently being built anywhere in the world," Sir James revealed. "In order to achieve this, we went together at our own expense to see every new theatre in Britain. Graham went to Scandinavia and America and I toured the majority of new opera houses in Germany at the invitation of the West German government. All this was done within two months of getting the commission and while the theatre was being designed. It had a significant effect on the design."

At the same time as it was pressing ahead with Eden Court, the Council was considering the future of the derelict Balnain House and deferred a decision to demolish it in order to enable Inverness Civic Trust to find a use for the building. The following month, the theatre's appeal committee decided to appoint a professional fund-raising company and Mrs Annie Rodgers, chairman of Inverness Amenities Association, set the ball rolling when she presented the first donation – £1000 from the proceeds of its summer entertainments.

In March, Hooker Craigmyle & Co was awarded the fund-raising contract and, two weeks later, Inverness's Playhouse Cinema was destroyed by fire, depriving the town of a facility that served as temporary theatre and concert hall. The following month, Graham Law and Sandy Dunbar were present when John Wyckham's plans were discussed in private by the Council and it was noted that the Bishop's Palace would be retained. It was agreed to make a public announcement the following week.

At the press conference, the project's estimated cost was said to be £627,000 with a second phase – a studio theatre – to be added later at a cost of £50,000. When it was finished,

Right
There was an instant marriage of minds when architect Graham Law joined John Wyckham on the Eden Court project team.

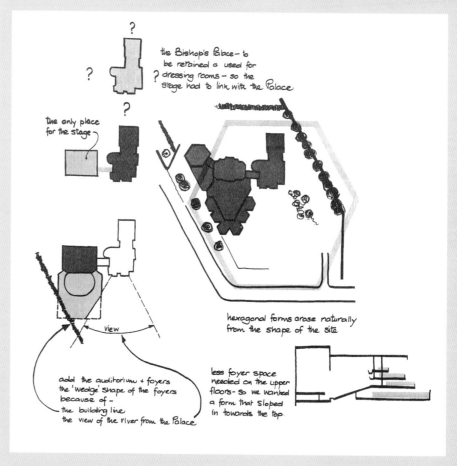

the Bishop's Palace – to be retained & used for dressing rooms – so the stage had to link with the Palace

the only place for the stage

hexagonal forms arose naturally from the shape of the site

view

add the auditorium & foyers the 'wedge' shape of the foyers because of – the building line the view of the river from the Palace

less foyer space needed on the upper floors – so we wanted a form that sloped in towards the top.

Above
Initial proposals of architect's plans and drawings for the new Eden Court Theatre

19

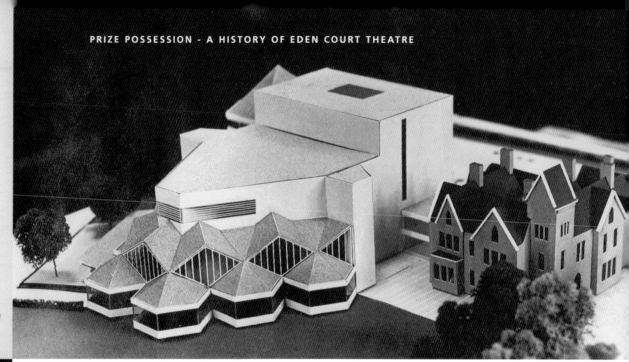

Right
The scale model of Eden Court Theatre built by Law & Dunbar-Nasmith offered Scottish Secretary Gordon Campbell a private view of what the Council was proposing.

Above
Clan Chief Sir Donald Cameron Of Lochiel headed the distinguished names on the newly-formed Eden Court Trust established to spearhead the public fund-raising campaign to which the Queen Mother contributed.

the theatre would be the finest in the country, Mr Law said. It would have 750-780 seats arranged in a horseshoe configuration, affording perfect sight-lines for every type of production. An additional 90 seats could be added for concerts and conferences. The stage would be designed for various uses from drama, opera and ballet to concerts and conferences and even dancing, with an orchestra pit for 50 musicians. Parking would be provided for 240 cars.

The consultant and architect returned to Inverness in September with drawings and a scale model and told the Council the scheme was now almost at the stage of making an application for planning approval.

In the interim, however, Harold Wilson's Labour Government had been defeated in a General Election and the new Scottish Secretary received a personal preview of the architect's plans for Eden Court at Holmrose, Croy, his private home near Inverness.

"I first became aware of the Council's plans for Eden Court as Shadow Secretary," The Rt. Hon. Gordon Campbell, now Lord Campbell Of Croy, said in 2001. "When I became Secretary of State For Scotland in June 1970, I was very much involved. I remember the Council wanted to get as much help as possible and I was able to obtain grants from the government through government agencies.

"James Dunbar-Nasmith was the brother of a very old friend of mine, Rear Admiral David Dunbar-Nasmith (who later became vice-chairman of the Highlands and Islands Development Board), who was exactly my age.

"James came to Inverness to see the Council on business and he brought a very large model of what was to become Eden Court – which included the Bishop's Palace – with him. When he came to visit us at Holmrose, I remember he set it up on our lawn so I could have a look. I was particularly interested to see what was going to be built and to learn it was not just going to be a theatre but had a whole lot of uses, which is what made the scheme such a boon to Inverness. It could not just accommodate pantomimes but visiting opera and ballet companies, conventions and conferences. Its multi-purposeness was just what was needed in Inverness."

Lord Campbell countered Council criticism that the rise in the cost of the theatre was due to delays in obtaining Scottish Office approval. "I don't remember any delay as far as Inverness was concerned," he said. "There was another project that had been going on even longer and never happened at all. That was the Edinburgh Opera House, a scheme that was going on at the same time as Eden Court."

In October, Inverness Opera Company donated £400 from its Little Theatre production of "The Pajama Game" to the Eden Court Appeal and the Scottish Development Department announced that no objections had been received to the statutory advertising of the project. Work could now proceed to tender with a view to starting in April. The HIDB and the SAC formally confirmed their grants of £150,000 each a few days later.

The Board congratulated Inverness Town Council on taking the initiative on such an imaginative project and was pleased the Scottish Secretary had granted its authority to make a substantial contribution to realising the Council's objective. Board Secretary Robert Fasken said: "From the outset, the Board have taken the view that the economic development now taking place in the Moray Firth area should be matched by improvements in the social and cultural facilities available. Eden Court will provide an admirable base for the growth of such activities in the area. It will also enhance the reputation of Inverness as a conference centre with consequent benefits to the town and its tourist industry."

Provost William Smith as chairman of the newly formed Eden Court Trust formally launched the Eden Court Appeal on 29th November 1972. Sir Donald Cameron Of Lochiel, Lord Lieutenant of Inverness-shire, was named as president and other members included the Lords Lieutenant of Ross & Cromarty and Nairn. The committee was completed by Town Clerk John Hill, Burgh Chamberlain Derek Bigg, Councillor Douglas Baxter, Inverness County Councillor Kenneth Walker, lawyer Robert Forrest, Nairn Provost Sandy Duncan and Margaret Young of Inverness Music Society.

Eden Court, the Provost stressed, was designed to enrich the cultural and social life of the Highlands and Lochiel added that the newly formed Trust was encouraged by the interest already shown throughout the North of Scotland. "The development is not needed just for the town but for the Highlands and its thousands of visitors," he declared. By way of illustration, it was announced that Inverness and Loch Ness Tourist Association had donated £500 to the appeal.

The soft-spoken Graham Law, a tall dark man with a military moustache and bearing, told the press conference that the seating capacity of Eden Court had now been fixed at 830 with a restaurant accommodating 200 people and the Bishop's Palace used for dressing rooms, wardrobe and offices. Building would start in March and be completed in November 1974.

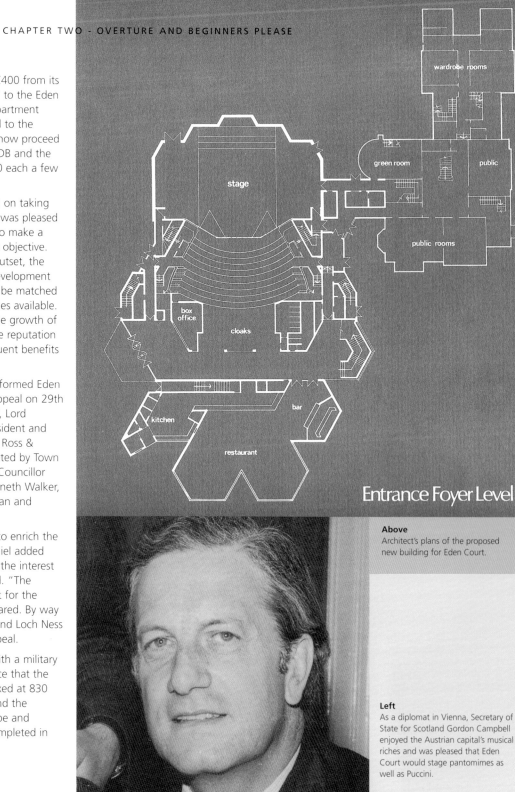

Entrance Foyer Level

Above
Architect's plans of the proposed new building for Eden Court.

Left
As a diplomat in Vienna, Secretary of State for Scotland Gordon Campbell enjoyed the Austrian capital's musical riches and was pleased that Eden Court would stage pantomimes as well as Puccini.

21

Left
The Award-winning Cathedral Players with cup and held by Mollie Hunter.

In his contribution to a promotional brochure, Law wrote: "One of our first problems was whether to retain or demolish the Palace. It could not be ignored… Any neighbour for such a building had to be tough and bold but, at the same time, sympathetic in design. We have tried to produce a design that expresses two things – the logic of the site and the logic of its function, which at the same time, respects the scale and form of its distinguished neighbours, the Palace and the Cathedral.

"If Eden Court fulfils its function, and if it merges quietly into its visual surroundings, we will have partially succeeded. If it gives the theatre-going public some indication that architects do try to grapple with the problems of the environment and that sense of 'occasion', then we will have succeeded even more".

In her leader of 1st December, Miss Barron said the Eden Court Appeal had a very good claim on the goodwill of all interested in promoting the arts in the Highlands. "Desirable,

Right
The Florians with the trophies they won. From left to right: George Dargavel, Marian Lindsay, Seumas Mackinnon, Carol Kane and Sandy Halley.

Left
A Florians production of
"Spring and Port Wine". Left to
right: Bobby Hepburn; Jimmy
Chisholm Jnr.; Marion Lindsay;
Callum Macdougall; Kitty Smith and
Biddy MacBean.

"WHAT EDEN COURT COURT MEANS TO ME"

PHIL CUNNINGHAM

"…it definitely gives credence to Scottish music…"

"The first time I played Eden Court was in the late 70s and now Aly Bain and I use it as the pinnacle of our Scottish tour every year. I've compered the annual schools show, "Rhythms Of The North", and I was very proud to perform my 'Highlands & Islands Suite' there. It's a big theatre and it definitely gives credence to Scottish music."

if not essential though a new auditorium in Inverness is for drama, opera, orchestras and other cultural entertainment, we still feel a much less ambitious project, to say nothing of something much less lavish than a professionally-run appeal with an expensive brochure, would be sufficient," she added.

"Furthermore, what on earth persuaded the Town Council, no doubt in order to encourage support from the counties, to bring onto the campaign committee three of HM Lieutenants, appointments which cut no ice whatsoever in Scotland, no matter how worthy its holders, when the county conveners would have been far more appropriate? It seems sheer stupidity to have by-passed the convener of Ross & Cromarty, the Earl Of Cromartie, whose interest in the arts, especially opera, is so well-known… and not to have had the Provost as principal committee-man is another piece of folly where a mainly Inverness project is concerned.

"Nevertheless, we hope the Trust will overcome these initial mistakes which could so easily have been avoided and that, although committed to an unnecessarily grandiose scheme, it will succeed – and may we add that we have already made a modest donation."

In the newspaper's correspondence columns, Miss Dorothy Urquhart of Wyvis Place, Inverness, welcomed the venture. "It should contribute an essential aesthetic quality to the Highland Capital lacking in past years and I wish it every success for the future," she declared.

Just before Christmas, Provost Smith announced that the Appeal had already raised £20,000. Eden Court was on its way – but some seeds of dissent had already been sown.

CHAPTER THREE

A HOUSE OF VANITY

The New Year began with the fulfilment of Councillor Douglas Baxter's prediction that Eden Court was a matter of national interest when the Scottish Tourist Board asked to meet Council representatives in Edinburgh to discuss the project. Some 100 contributions had now been received to the appeal, which stood at £24,330 but, reflecting the slight adjustment in the cost of Eden Court, the amount to be raised was now £85,000.

The public was also beginning to make its views known. Plans for the theatre were now on public display in the Town House and on 23rd January a letter appeared in the Courier from D. R. MacDonald of Druim Avenue, Inverness, who wrote: "Inspecting the model of Eden Court, I was appalled to find it appeared to have been designed by an idiot child on a psychedelic trip. If it were sited in the vicinity of the gasworks, it would be bad enough but at least it might harmonise with its surroundings. The proposed site, however, shows such a lack of good taste and aesthetic sense that the mind boggles. It is the desecration of a beautiful riverside area and a holy place."

J. H. Martin of Carrbridge concurred. "I do not agree with the statement in the brochure that it harmonises with the surrounding architecture. In my view, the frontage is too fussy for the site," he wrote. "It appears to me that the restaurant is badly placed side by side with the main entrance with all the disadvantages of noise, smell and traffic."

In March, Councillor Baxter announced that although he had another year to serve, he intended to stand down in May. He enjoyed Council work but found it demanding and had decided not to continue. Provost Smith expressed his regret and said he would pay proper tribute to his colleague in May. What many of his colleagues did not know was that Councillor Baxter was suffering from cancer.

Ten days later, Provost Smith revealed that the cost of Eden Court had increased considerably and announced that donors to the Appeal included the Queen Mother who had a home in Caithness. "This contribution, more than anything, confirms the importance to the whole Highlands of this project," he declared.

The Appeal now stood at £77,011 and the Provost had decided to write an open letter to the public, urging them to help push the total towards – or even beyond – its original target. "We are now in a period of rapidly rising building costs and will have to pay a lot more than we were originally anticipating for the theatre which, as a result of the considerably increased population in the area, is all the more needed," he stated. "It is therefore essential that the public raises as much as possible."

Significantly, the Provost did not reveal the extent of the increase in the cost of Eden Court. This failure to take the public into the Council's confidence would dog Eden Court and harden attitudes against it.

On 26th March, 1973, Inverness Town Council held a special meeting to determine whether to proceed with Eden Court in the light of soaring costs and it emerged that the complex would now cost £1.3m. The Council was told that the Scottish Secretary was "very disappointed" and it was warned that no increase in grant could be expected beyond the declared 50% of the original estimate of £600,000. He suggested the Council devise a more modest scheme or defer the project.

Provost Smith, Treasurer William Fraser, Town Clerk John R. Hill and Town Chamberlain Derek Bigg had already met to discuss the crisis, however.

Left
Work begins at last – Provost William Smith cuts the first sod at Eden Court on 10th May 1973 and an objector performed a similar ceremony on the Provost's front lawn.

Left
Treasurer William Fraser, later Provost of Inverness, attended the crisis briefing that was told the lowest tender for Eden Court was twice as high as expected.

Right
Labour councillor Tom MacKenzie donated to the Eden Court Appeal but grew alarmed at the rise in cost and supported the move to abandon the project.

Left
The special Council meeting of 26th March 1973 was the defining moment for Eden Court and for Inverness, Councillor Ron Lyon recalled.

"Derek calculated that, on his best estimate, we could proceed without breaching the limit we could statutorily spend on arts and entertainment and not be liable for the surcharge the Secretary Of State would otherwise be obliged to impose on the councillors," Treasurer, now ex-Provost, Fraser recalled. "With his tongue in his cheek, John R. Hill, said: 'I must advise you not to accept this tender because you don't have borrowing consent from the Secretary Of State - but I've got to remind you of the consequences if you don't accept it.'

"We were aware that some members of the council were afraid of being surcharged but, having gone through the sums with Derek Bigg to satisfy myself that his projections were realistic and his calculations were correct, as I knew they would be – Derek was a man of great ability and vision, seeing the future of computers before anyone else – I was confident that we could accept it without incurring a penalty. We decided to recommend that the tender should be accepted – and with the exception of three members, the Council was with us all the way."

Backed by his Labour Party colleagues Dan Corbett and Tom MacKenzie who had donated to the Appeal, Councillor James Cameron moved that the arts complex plan be abandoned but Provost Smith proposed an amendment, seconded by Treasurer William Fraser, that the scheme should proceed and the Council should negotiate with the Scottish Office for an increase in borrowing consent. To abandon the project would break faith with many people and lose the opportunity to provide a much-needed cultural facility for Inverness and the Highlands, the Provost declared.

He reminded the council they were building for the future and if they decided not to proceed before the March 31st deadline set by the Scottish Secretary, they would have to start all over again with a new and less expensive scheme. If, on the other hand, they decided to modify the existing project, there would be more delay, the result would be unsatisfactory and, at the speed prices were rising, the cost would probably be even greater.

He was confident they could get more money from the Secretary Of State, as Edinburgh had done for its proposed opera house, and there were also other people willing to contribute.

The seriousness of the situation was reflected in the decision to move to a roll call vote with the Provost winning by a majority of more than 4:1. His bold move was backed by Bailies Iain Fraser, Bob King, Alistair Milne and Douglas Baxter, Police Judge Kenneth Macleod, Treasurer Fraser and his wife, Councillor Margaret Fraser and Councillors Mabel Skinner, Ron Lyon, Allan Sellar, Bud Cameron, Ritchie MacPhee, Gordon Campbell and Gerald Pollitt. Dean Of Guild Peter Drummond was absent.

"There was a terrible sense of crisis; Eden Court was on a knife edge," Councillor Lyon recalled. "I remember being told, if you incur expenditure without the Scottish Secretary's authority, the members of the Council could be surcharged – and it was an enormous sum – but I voted firmly to proceed.

"I said at the time that this was the defining moment. Either Inverness stays a cow town on the fringes of everything or it becomes a proper town with modern amenities. I'm not a patron of the arts but my impression was that a theatre had a civilising influence on the population of a town and people coming in to live and work would be accustomed to having facilities like Eden Court was going to provide. It would raise the tone of the place.

"The thing about Eden Court was that there were two guys on the Council – Baxter and Smith – neither of whom I had much time for, but they deserve their place in local history," Councillor Lyon added. "Baxter had a knowledge of the arts

and the ideas; Smith was a businessman and he had the political muscle. He was a very forceful character.

"They had nerves of steel, the pair of them, Bill Smith especially. He just wouldn't back down. He would say we have to do it and everybody else would fall in line but I'm sure John R. Hill would be working away behind the scenes. He wasn't afraid to speak out and I don't think the Provost or Treasurer would have gone ahead without the Scottish Secretary's approval against the advice of the Town Clerk or Town Chamberlain.

"There wasn't this consensus approach. There was no focus group or consultation process with Smith or Baxter. They just went out and laid it on the line: 'Either we go for bust or we don't get it' – and the way things have turned out, it was the right decision to take!"

John Wyckham was in attendance for that meeting. "The Labour councillors wanted to turn it into a warehouse or something," he chuckled. "And Mabel Skinner, the Communist Councillor, actually sided with the Conservatives on the council vote to proceed. I went up to her afterwards and gave her a hug and said, 'Mabel, I can't believe you didn't vote with Labour' and she said, 'Well, I'd never heard so much tommyrot in all my life!'"

Left
"Art is for everyone" was Communist councillor Mabel Skinner's battle cry. She didn't see Eden Court as exclusively for an elite and championed education and access for all.

"WHAT EDEN COURT COURT MEANS TO ME"

RUSSELL HUNTER

"...it was such a heady adventure opening a new theatre in Inverness..."

"It was such a heady adventure opening a new theatre in Inverness. I was never in love with the old Empire but I enjoyed playing there because I enjoyed playing to the people. Eden Court is a fun theatre to play because you get an honest reaction from the audience – unlike some places I know where you are playing to, if you'll pardon the expression, blue rinses and it's very easy to upset them by stepping over their line. You go into the bar and there's people with white hair, grey hair, blue hair and purple hair. You don't find that at Eden Court."

The Courier reporting the meeting also carried an editorial which noted: "In these inflationary days, it can surprise no-one that the estimated cost of Eden Court has doubled. We have no doubt that a new theatre and concert hall is badly needed in Inverness but the one proposed is, to us, far too grand and ambitious and now far too expensive."

"I never had any doubt that we were doing the right thing," ex-Treasurer Fraser commented in 2001. "If we hadn't taken the bull by the horns that night, we wouldn't have a theatre today.

"It might have been built for £630,000 if we'd got the green light straight away but, by the time we got the go-ahead, inflation was rampant and, while we were disturbed that the cost of the project had doubled, we were in no doubt that the Scottish Office would be aware of the reason why – and that if we had deferred a decision, the price would have risen even higher and we wouldn't have been able to afford it."

"It was a very worrying time," Bigg added. "Having the Council base its decision on my calculations was a big responsibility to bear."

Recalling events of more than a quarter of a century earlier Lord Campbell, who had approved the project at £630,000, expressed no surprise that the tender price had doubled. "That was to be expected," he commented. "I'm surprised it hadn't trebled."

With the Council's historic vote, public outrage erupted in the columns of the Courier.

In a light-hearted letter of 10th April 1974, William MacKay of Hawthorn Drive raised some serious issues. "It came as a big surprise to me to see that four-fifths of the people (on the Council) are in favour of the grand and costly new building at Eden Court provided for future generations at the expense of the present tax-soaked people. Wow, a regular Taj Mahal, but I suppose we can't stop the hand of progress... I ponder the final cost... and I haven't a clue what the running costs of such an elite establishment would be."

A regular correspondent to the Courier, Ewan A. MacQueen switched his concerns from the Common Market and, in his opening attack, congratulated Councillors Cameron, Corbett and MacKenzie on their wisdom and courage. "If spared and well, the cost in these days of inflation will have topped the £2m mark by the end of this year," he predicted. "It is certainly a staggering sum for a house of vanity and is undoubtedly a merciless and unprofitable burden on the town of Inverness."

"Last autumn we were reminded in your columns of the destruction by fire of previous theatres in the town (the Theatre Royal and the Playhouse). It looks now as if history is to be ignored and yet another theatre is to be built on ground consecrated for the worship of God (a reference to the chapel in the Bishop's Palace). It is written: 'Thou shalt not tempt the Lord thy God'."

If "house of vanity" became a popular if rather ironically-used synonym for Eden Court, "Ratepayer" had another in the same issue. He – or she – praised the three dissenting councillors as sensible men. "Surely there are others who will join us. The whole scheme has never been popular but at £600,000, people were prepared to accept it. Now, at over £1 m, most people are not. Inverness is not a large town and certainly not large enough to be burdened with this white elephant.

"Let the council take another close look and then decide to scrap the project in anything like its present form. The police will be out of Farraline Park in about two years. The fabric of the building they share with the Little Theatre is sound and there is no reason why the inside

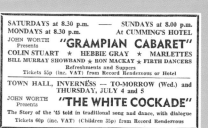

Left
Newspaper advertisements for 1969-74 events.

should not be reconstructed at not as high a cost to give us a really good theatre of a size which would suit Inverness which has never been very theatre-minded."

The argument equating sport with fitness and art with frivolity entered the debate with a letter from "Sportswoman". "I would not suggest the town does not need a theatre but it surely has a very limited appeal," she wrote. "It will only be able to seat 800 people and at £1.3 million that works out at £1685 per seat. Already I've heard someone on the bus call it 'Smith's Folly' and it certainly seems like it. Yet it was him that stopped the idea of a sports centre in the town a few years ago, if I remember rightly, at a fraction of the cost. This would have catered for a lot more people and I know my own sport of badminton would have benefited enormously. It appears to be that the Town Council favour music for the minority to muscles for the masses."

The following week the Council raised council house rents and a Courier correspondent, "Icarus", branded Mr MacQueen – a son of the Free Presbyterian manse – an anachronism. "He calls the Eden Court centre a 'house of vanity' and talks at some length about desecration of God's ground. Mr MacQueen would do well to remember Swift's words: 'We have just enough religion to hate but not enough to love one another'."

"If the Eden Court centre were to cost £5m it would be a bargain. This to Bailie Cameron and his Philistine colleagues who bring everything down to terms of hard cash. Without ignoring the practicalities of cost and inflation, there are many of us who believe deeply in the high value of an arts centre in Inverness."

Another correspondent hailed a redeveloped Farraline Park as the common-sense solution. "Let us consider what free capital we have before borrowing on the strength of future generations," he or she wrote. "Even one dressed stone of Victorian vintage speaks more of art and craft than any prefabricated structure purposefully designed to be obsolete before completion."

"Resident" entered the lists alleging that Provost Smith had been covering up the true increase in the cost of Eden Court and that far from there being no objections, there had been one objection. He expressed the hope that impending regionalisation of local government would bring changes for the better.

The Provost was stung into a reply on 27th April. "Some of the criticism is constructive, some amusing and, alas, some merely carping and destructive," he wrote. "We welcome constructive criticism but destructive and mischievous criticism

Above
TV personality Jimmy Saville's exploits on Ben Nevis had given him an attachment to the Highlands and he was invited to join Eden Court's management committee.

is not worthy of reply. It is noted that your correspondents hide behind pseudonyms, with the exception of Mr MacQueen for whom I have a very great personal regard and respect although not necessarily agreeing with him.

"'Resident' impugned the integrity of the Council and names myself and the Treasurer in particular. I strongly refute this individual's charges of dishonesty. At every stage of the Eden Court saga, which has lasted four years, the information given was in accordance with the facts before us at the time.

"On the general question, I appreciate that is controversial and I am prepared to meet any representative body of objectors and reply to criticism. I also appreciate that many opposing views are sincerely held. Alas too much criticism is merely mischievous.

"Finally I suggest those who deplore this burden on the rates to do a simple arithmetical exercise which will reveal to them the cost of Eden Court and I pose the question: 'Is 2p on the net rateable assessment too great a price to pay for a centre which will fill a long-felt want in the Capital of the Highlands for generations to come?'

"The Town Council has taken a courageous and, in my opinion, correct step. I fancy that far from being reviled in the future as 'a millstone', 'a continuing burden' and other uncomplimentary names, Eden Court will indeed be a memorial in the best sense of the word to the farsightedness and the courage of the present council to enrich the good way of life in Inverness and the Highlands."

Time would prove him right – and the Courier offered a measure of sympathy, noting in its editorial that it was the lot of councils everywhere to be an Aunt Sally. "Perhaps the Council's answer would be the comment of the old Scotsman tired of being advised how to deal with his nagging spouse: 'Aye, aye. Everybody knows what to do with a coorse wife, except him that has her!'"

At the Council meeting on 1st May, Councillor Lyon, then a reporter with a national newspaper, expressed concern at what he called unnecessary confidentiality applied to Council discussions about Eden Court and was smacked down by Councillor Baxter who reminded him that the final decision on Eden Court had been conducted in open session and the full and frank debate had been reported by the press. The reason for holding discussions in private had been because "personalities were involved" and discussion would have been inhibited, he added.

Councillor Lyon could not be accused of looking after the interests of his professional colleagues, however. At a meeting of the local branch of the National Union Of Journalists, he submitted a motion deploring the standard of reporting of council meetings. Unsurprisingly, he did not obtain a seconder.

The meeting then went on to consider who should be nominated for the new theatre's Board of Governors. Names included local people associated with the arts including Peter Donald, managing director of Inverness Motor Company and secretary of Inverness Music Society, Councillor Baxter, Bailie Alistair Milne – and Jimmy Savile who had developed close ties with Fort William after being rescued from Ben Nevis by Lochaber Mountain Rescue Team.

The radio and TV personality declined, however, and even Councillor Milne had reservations about accepting. "I told Douglas I couldn't serve on his committee because my sole experience of the theatre was confined to going to see 'Annie Get Your Gun' when I was doing National Service in London," he recalled. Douglas said: "I don't want your aesthetic knowledge, I want your vote!"

Despite the criticism levelled at him in the Courier's correspondence columns, Provost Smith was re-elected in the Council elections of May 1973 and re-appointed Provost. On 7th May, 1973, Inverness Town Council applied to the Secretary of State to borrow some £800,000 to meet the increase in the cost of Eden Court.

In the Courier, Flora Gowans of Attadale Road leapt to defend Mr MacQueen – "an enlightened man"– from Icarus's onslaught. "I would agree Inverness needs a suitable cultural centre but one that will cost more than £1 m is superfluous to basic requirements," she added. "Raigmore Hospital complex remains incomplete and that £1 m would go a long way to seeing a functional part of it in operation."

Mr MacQueen recalled that Inverness Town Council had been offered the Empire Theatre for £40,000 and turned it down. "Doesn't Icarus know that places of entertainment are fast disappearing from our towns and cities," he said. "Already 70% of actors and actresses unemployed. In the past 25 years, the number of cinemas has been reduced from 4500 to 1500 because television has brought entertainment into the homes of all who want it? Therefore vast public expenditure on a theatre appears to be totally unnecessary.

'Doesn't Icarus know that Aviemore is now the conference and entertainment centre of the Highlands and that it is striving desperately to try and pay its way? Inverness Town Council should progress works of greater benefit to the welfare of the town and ease the acute housing shortage."

"Resident" added his voice, calling on the Provost to address his unanswered questions and William MacKay returned to the fray to accuse the Provost of assuming the role of Big Daddy to future generations when today's teenagers had nowhere to go.

Ceremonially cutting the first sod on 10th May, enabling Crudens the contractors to start work, Provost Smith said it was a red-letter day in the history of the town and he welcomed the full support expressed by the new chairman of the HIDB, Sir Andrew Gilchrist. The four-year Scottish Office delay in approving public money for the project accounted for the escalation in cost, he said, but he was confident there would be no further delays and work would be completed in 18-24 months.

In "Historic Inverness", Gerald Pollitt recalled that after the first sod had been cut at Eden Court, a still-persistent objector to the theatre had protested by performing a similar ceremony on Provost Smith's front lawn.

The first meeting of Eden Court's new management committee took place that day. It was now chaired by Peter Donald and comprised Inverness District Councillors Peter Drummond and Alistair Milne, Scottish Community Drama Association (SCDA) chairman Lindsay Hamilton, Lady Gilchrist, Margaret Young, SCDA adviser Graham Souter and retired bank manager Bill Hunter.

In the Courier, Margaret Urquhart of St Valery Avenue said Eden Court would be no more a house of vanity than the cathedral. "It would be a place where people could use the gifts God gave them and charities could benefit," she declared and, in the same issue, "Icarus", revealing himself as Niall Duncan MacKillop of Cantraybruich Farm, Culloden Moor, echoed Mrs Urquhart's theme. Eden Court, he said would teach young people to appreciate art and beauty, encourage laughter and reflect on the ways of humanity.

Meanwhile, the town's artistic life continued in *ad hoc* venues. The National Mod of 1972 had been held in The Playhouse before the fire, chart-topping groups like Love Affair and The Sweet played in the Caledonian Ballroom, The Corries in the Town Hall, Billy Connolly at the Cummings Hotel, 7:84's trail-blazing "The Cheviot, The Stag And The Black, Black Oil" in The Little Theatre, Inverness Choral Society in St Columba's Church and jazz and folk groups in various lounge bars.

Although work was by now progressing on site at Eden Court, Mr MacQueen maintained his opposition to the project. "No valid reasons can be given for granting public

Above
"I don't want your aesthetic knowledge, I want your vote," Councillor Baxter said when he proposed Council colleague Alistair Milne for his Eden Court committee.

money for a house of vanity before the redevelopment of Dempster Gardens, 2 car parks, 6000-7000 houses and empty spaces in Huntly Street, King Street, Celt Street and the Merkinch area," he wrote. "In any Christian society it was always understood that works of necessity and mercy took precedence over frivolity and the denial of a thrifty heritage and having the loving advice of the scriptural truth was always welcome."

Another classical scholar, "Aristides" deplored the Provost's declaration that Eden Court would go on with no withdrawal whatsoever. He recalled that the Town Council's coat of arms could not be more appropriate – "The white elephant will break the camel's back," he declared.

Despite the concerns of Mrs Gowans and Mr MacQueen, other public works were taking place in Inverness. A post-graduate medical centre had been opened at Raigmore and a £9m hospital expansion had been approved.

For financial reasons, the Council decided to turn down a request to twin with a Japanese town, which put one Courier reader in mind of "The Mikado" and in the Courier's correspondence columns of 5th June, "Savoyard" burst into song, providing readers with a Gilbertian source of innocent merriment:

> "In a place by the river, we're going to commit
> Oh, millions and millions and millions
> And I said to the Council 'Oh Why do you sit
> Spending millions and millions and millions?
> 'Is it weakness of intellect?' loudly I cried
> "Or delusions of grandeur that you've got inside?'
> With a shake of their poor little heads they replied
> 'Oh millions and millions and millions.'
> Now I feel just as sure as I'm sure that my name
> Isn't 'millions and millions and millions.'
> That t'was misplaced ambition that made them exclaim
> 'Oh millions and millions and millions. '
> The cost started high and each day it inflates
> And any objectors are classed as ingrates
> But just think what it's going to put on the rates —
> Oh millions and millions and millions!"

In the same issue, "Resident" was still nipping at the Provost's heels and yapping for answers. He also noted the Council's sense of urgency in starting the work. "Could this be perhaps construed as an effort to force the Scottish Secretary's hand

into giving the money for this extravagant project?" he asked. "One would hope that a little ice from the Chancellor's freeze on public spending might form on Eden Court."

Nairn District Council had decided to donate £1000 to the Eden Court Appeal and a local ratepayer objected, maintaining that the money should have gone on a local amenity but the Council re-affirmed its decision as contributing to a project that would benefit Nairn.

Later that month, the Council considered names for the new complex and rejected the Royal Highland Theatre. It would not be just a theatre, Provost Smith said. He suggested it should be known simply as Eden Court. "Sadler's Wells and Covent Garden are known by these names."

"Resident" choked on his Sugar Frosties when he read that and, in the Courier of 26th June, revealed himself to be Andrew J. MacDonald of Ballifeary Road, a 20 year old accountancy trainee, a former member of the Inverness Royal Academy team that had been runners-up TV's "Top Of The Form" a few years earlier, and a vociferous Young Conservative, leading to the suspicion among some councillors that he was providing a mouthpiece for a prominent Tory who lived opposite Eden Court.

"Your report confirms what I have long suspected – that the Provost of Inverness suffers from delusions of grandeur," Mr MacDonald wrote. "What else could prompt him to liken this pitiful cultural effort with Sadler's Wells or Covent Garden? In London, any theatre has a catchment area of 15m people whereas Inverness, at most has 60,000 and, if Covent Garden needs subsidising by government grants with its huge audience potential, I pity the ratepayers of Inverness.

"On the question of finance, there is one significant fact which Provost Smith and Treasurer Fraser have so far concealed from fellow councillors and from electors. No-one has yet been officially informed of the survey carried out by a firm of theatre consultants into the Eden Court project which resulted in the following costing: at 80% utilisation, it will run at a deficit of £50,000 per annum. I need hardly say more, except to add that even a 30% utilisation figure for 'Smith's Folly' would be an optimistic assumption."

Charles Bannerman, a student teacher and a prominent local athlete, accused his former "Top Of the Form" team-mate of inconsistency, criticising Eden Court for being "too large" while belittling it as "pitiful" and for being guilty of the same sin as he accused the Provost and Treasurer – of concealing knowledge of the consultant's report. There were many theatres in London competing for the potential audience of 15m and Covent Garden productions were much more expensive than those likely to be staged at Eden Court, he added.

He and the majority of local folk had every confidence in Provost Smith and Treasurer Fraser. "It's high time people stopped playing politics and, like those on the Town Council who are in favour of such a project, began to think constructively about what is best for the town." he stated.

Possibly with a view to selling land to meet the additional cost of Eden Court, the Council decided to offer ground adjacent to the theatre/conference complex for a hotel of up to 100 bedrooms and there were several replies but the Town did not own enough ground and the County Council refused to sell an adjoining site earmarked for a primary school.

The exchange of letters continued in the Courier through August with "A Theatregoer" pointing out that the town did not adequately support music and drama events already being staged in the town and questioning if Eden Court would fare any better.

In September, the Council appointed two pupils as youth representatives to the theatre's management committee and, as the entire country looked forward to the grimmer reality of a three-day week, the newspaper debate fizzled out – no doubt, much to the Council and Board's relief.

Inverness continued to expand, however. Plans were announced for a massive redevelopment of Eastgate and a page of letters carried by the Courier on 18th December did not contain one about Eden Court. Messrs MacQueen and MacDonald had been silent for some months – but they had not given up the fight.

They had found an even more effective way of opposing Eden Court than writing to the Courier and it would send shock waves reverberating round the Town House early in the New Year.

Above
Dancing teacher, choreographer at the Empire and creator of the annual "Merry Go Round" at Eden Court, Margaret Firth MBE on her retirement in 1995.

Below
Andrew Bremner and Louise Munro in a dramatic scene from the Florians much-talked about production of "Maria Martin" in 1975.

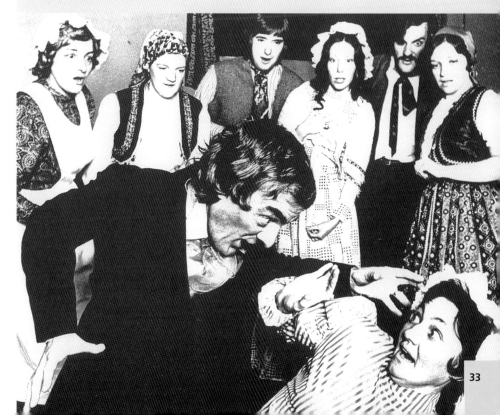

CHAPTER FOUR

MONEY, MONEY, MONEY

The Town Council broke all records for lengthy sittings when it re-assembled in 4th January 1974. Eden Court's steel contractors had gone bankrupt and in a desperate effort to avoid another costly delay, the Council held crisis talks with theatre consultant, architect and site quantity surveyor, Derek Gardiner of Souter & Jaffrey.

Councillor James Cameron unsuccessfully moved that the matter be discussed in public. "There has been too much talk about Eden Court behind closed doors," he declared. The Provost pointed out that the discussion would involve prices, personalities and contractual matters and confidentiality was essential. A public statement issued after the meeting revealed that the architect had been asked to report back to the Council within four weeks.

The Council also heard that Inverness County Council's Education Department no longer required the land at the Cathedral Car Park for a school and would be prepared to sell it, with the agreement of the church authorities who had given it to them for that purpose.

Meanwhile the development of Inverness carried on apace with McDermott's oil platform construction yard at Ardersier and an Ice Rink at the Bught Park. Plans were also approved for housing an expanding population in major housing estates at Smithton, Culloden and Balloch, that would have an estimated population of 15,000. The Inverness Music Society met in The Little Theatre for a concert by the London Virtuosi featuring a flautist called James Galway.

In March, the three-day week led to a change of Government. Labour took power and the formidable Willie Ross returned as Scottish Secretary. The Rotary Club presented the Council with £600 for the Eden Court Appeal which now topped £100,000 – but a few, days later the Provost, who was 73, was admitted to hospital.

Councillor Alistair Milne took the chair when the Council met again on 26th March and, after hearing from the Eden Court project team leaders, appointed replacement steel contractors, discussing in private, related contingency and contractual matters that would have to be negotiated with Crudens and the new steel erectors.

The Council was also given a statement on the full construction costs to date and expressed its satisfaction that the need to bring in new steel contractors had not materially affected costs.

A rare insight into the subsequent reaction in St Andrew's House was afforded by Sir James Dunbar-Nasmith in 2001. "It was actually at a meeting with Bob Butler, the Scottish Office official responsible, attended by Provost Smith, John Hill, John Wyckham, Graham Law and myself. John Hill told Butler that, in spite of the Scottish Office attitude to the cost of tenders, we were going to go ahead. 'I can't send the Queen Mother's money back,' he said – and stormed out."

Hill's volatility was well-known in St Andrew's House where civil servants were warned to handle him with care but the pressure on Council representatives to abandon Eden Court became increasingly intense.

"John met Lord Polwarth, the Minister of State at the Scottish Office, who asked if he was prepared to go to prison," the former Town Clerk's widow, Isla, recalled. "John laughed – but I didn't laugh when he came home and told me. He said there was no way they could send him to prison. He knew the Scottish Office had to accept the situation and give the Council the money they needed to finish the building because if they made the Council wait, it was going to cost even more."

Above
Shrewd and determined, Inverness Town Clerk John R Hill played a leading part in convincing the Council that it could proceed with Eden Court before it received borrowing consent from the Scottish Office.

Left
Inverness Town Council's steely resolve to proceed with Eden Court Theatre was shaken when their steel contractor went into liquidation. A replacement – and a source of steel – proved hard to find in the prevailing economic climate.

Right
Provost Ian Fraser who chaired
the first Inverness District Council
and, later, the theatre's Board
Of Governors.

"John risked his reputation by advising the Council to go ahead – but he felt they had spent so much and the building was so advanced, the only option was to finish it without delay."

"He was very interested in the arts and thought that Eden Court would be good for Inverness and the Highlands," Mrs Hill added. "He took a great interest in the technical side of the project because it was so different from the legal and contractual work he was involved in.

"I've no doubt Provost Smith threw his weight behind the proposal to proceed as a result of John's advice and I was so mad when they didn't invite him to the opening. He'd taken up a new appointment in Ayr by that time. Provost Smith got all the credit for Eden Court, but it would never have been built if it wasn't for John and Douglas Baxter."

Looking frailer, the Provost returned to Council duties at the beginning of April and the following week, members considered Eden Court Management Committee's request to proceed with arrangements for the centre's opening concert. Bailie Peter Drummond said artists had to be booked up to 18 months in advance and it was agreed that the first week's programme should cater for a wide range of tastes.

The Council also noted that the church authorities were opposed to the adjoining ground being sold and that the hotel development was therefore unlikely to go ahead.

The following month, elections were held for the new district and regional authorities that were to replace the existing structure of town and county councils. Provost Smith and a number of his Town Council colleagues stood and were successful at the polls. The District councillors would "shadow" the Town for a year.

On 12th May, Councillor David Murray moved that in view of the increase in cost, the Town Council investigate the possibility of Eden Court being sold to a private operator, not necessarily for the same purpose. "Like many other people in the town, I'm concerned about the cost of the project," he said. "I realise my proposal will present problems but I feel it should be investigated." He was seconded by Councillor Cameron who felt it was time for the matter to be reviewed. Treasurer Fraser said the Council had spent many hours discussing Eden Court and the subject had been thoroughly aired. There was no point in going over the ground again. The motion was defeated by 14 votes to five.

The following week, Caledonia House, a multi-storey office block built on the site of the Empire, was opened.

On Monday 2nd June, councillors watching the Grampian TV News froze over their fish fingers. In what looks with hindsight like an enterprising piece of investigative journalism, the bulletin carried a story that the Scottish Secretary had ordered an inquiry into the Council's application to borrow £800,000 to meet the rise in the project's costs. Councillors were incensed when they met that night. Town Clerk John Hill reported that he had received no notification. The deadline for withdrawing objections had been 1st June and he had received no information on whether any had been withdrawn. The application for borrowing consent had been lodged 18 months earlier and publicly advertised for objections.

On 7th June, the Courier carried the formal announcement that two objections – one with a petition containing 91 signatures – had been received against the Council's application and the next step would be a public inquiry. The following Wednesday, a special Town Council meeting was held and it decided to write to the Scottish Secretary seeking a meeting before a date was set for the public inquiry. Mr Hill revealed he had yet to receive official notification from the Scottish Office.

Treasurer Fraser said it was wrong that the news should break in the media before the Council had been told and the Provost bitterly criticised the Scottish Office for its handling of the matter. "The Council has been treated shamefully and the time has come to attack," he declared.

He maintained the increase in the cost of the project had arisen while the Scottish Office had been considering the matter. "In May we were told that if two objections to the scheme were not withdrawn by June there would be a public inquiry," he said. "Although the fact that there will now be a public inquiry has been released through the news media, we have had no notification at all. We do not even know who the objectors are because the Scottish Office has withheld these names.

"There must be no shilly-shallying. We must now give dates that indicate the long waits for departmental approval which have caused costs to escalate. I'm forced to the conclusion it is the permanent officials at the Scottish Office that are at fault.

"I welcome a public inquiry where all the facts will be revealed, showing that the escalating costs is not the fault of the Town Council and it will show the Scottish Office in a poor light," he added.

Councillor Iain Fraser suggested that the Council should enlist the support of North MPs and ask them to approach the Scottish Secretary.

In view of the situation, the Council's Finance Committee deferred a decision on spending £6,234 on a grand piano for Eden Court until after the public inquiry.

The Council's bid to forestall the hearing was frustrated when the Scottish Secretary declined to meet them because he had already decided to hold the inquiry, which had been fixed for 24th September. On 29th July, the Council agreed to brief legal counsel but the Provost complained that the Council had still not been advised who the objectors were or the nature of their objections.

Two days later, the "shadow" Inverness District Council met for the first time and elected Councillor Iain Fraser as Provost in a remarkable manner. Having tied with Councillor William Fraser, his was the name drawn from the hat.

The following month Miss Barron made her annual visit to the Edinburgh International Festival and found herself in a parallel universe. As she reported to the Courier: "Eden Court is small fry compared to Edinburgh's opera house project but there are certain similarities. Like Inverness, Edinburgh Council met with strong opposition and there had been considerable debate over the years. Like its Inverness counterpart, Edinburgh Council maintained it was the only site and would meet the mounting need for a centre for the performing arts, not just opera, the name 'opera' having given the impression it was being designed for an elite."

Left
A man of principle and much liked by his pupils, technical teacher Ewan MacQueen maintained a steadfast opposition to Eden Court on religious and financial grounds, writing to the Courier and lodging a formal objection to the Council's application for borrowing consent.

The proposed opera house – which, unlike Eden court, never came into being, was to hold 1400 people and cost £1.8m.

At the festival, Miss Barron attended a new opera based on the life of Cromarty stonemason and geologist, Courier correspondent and author, Hugh Miller written by Reginald Barratt Ayres of Aberdeen University's music department to a libretto by Colin MacLean. Something worth reviving today at Eden Court?

Ewan MacQueen – who, it was to emerge, had been one of the objectors who had caused the public inquiry – reappeared in print, but this time in the Courier's Public Notices column on 10th September. "As I have been asked to grant an opportunity to objectors to sign their names witnessing against the folly, the enormous expense (£120,000 extra on the rates per year) and the sinful influence of the proposed Eden Court Theatre, the papers may be signed at the YMCA, Bank Street from Tuesday-Friday 10th-13th September," he announced.

Two weeks before the second general election of the year, the public inquiry into Eden Court opened in Inverness Town House. It was conducted by Sir Alan Hume, Edinburgh. To no one's surprise, the objectors were Mr MacQueen, represented by Mr J R Fiddes QC, and Mr MacDonald who represented himself. Mr A M Morrison QC represented the Council.

Mr Morrison said that in 1972 the Scottish Secretary had approved the Town Council's application to borrow £250,000 for their share of Eden Court's building costs, based on the estimates at that time. There had been one objector but the Scottish Secretary decided it was not serious enough to warrant a public inquiry and had, in fact, dismissed it as "frivolous". By 1973 the building costs had increased considerably from £620,000 to £1,300,000, the QC went on. The Highland Board had issued a statement acknowledging their awareness of the situation and expressing their anxiety that the project should get under way. The Board maintained that the economic developments taking place in the Moray Firth area should be matched by social and cultural facilities.

Right
His activities with the Young Conservatives gave Andrew MacDonald the reputation of a 'gadfly'. His objections certainly irritated Provost William Smith.

Accordingly, the Council had chosen to go ahead on the basis of tenders, without obtaining borrowing consent as further delay could have meant that the cost would become prohibitive, Mr Morrison went on. The fact that the Scottish Secretary had already approved borrowing of £250,000 and dismissed the earlier objection as frivolous seemed to indicate to the Council that the Scottish Secretary approved of the project in general. The decision meant they were able to obtain a favourable fixed-price contract. The difference between £600,000 and £1,300,000 might seem large but it still represented extremely good value for money, the QC added.

"The fact remains that expenditure has been incurred. There is no serious question of the project being abandoned. The question that arises is whether the expenditure should be financed by loan. The alternative would be that expenditure is carried forward and handed over to the District Council when it takes over next year.

"The project is supported by large numbers of responsible people and organisations, it is good value for money and its effect on the rates would not be excessive," he added, pointing out it was permissible for local authorities to incur expenditure of up to 2.5p on the rates for cultural purposes and that the existing legislation would soon be replaced in favour of making it "the duty of local authorities to make adequate provision for cultural and recreational facilities".

Town Chamberlain Derek Bigg – who was questioned for more than two hours – told the Inquiry Reporter that the £75,000 which the Scottish Secretary had decreed be raised by public subscription had been exceeded. The appeal currently stood at £102,000 with donations from 93 corporate bodies and 342 individuals, including £44,700 from neighbouring councils. The total expenditure so far on Eden Court amounted to £630,061, he added, and maintained that the limit of 2.5p on the rates had never been exceeded. He calculated the rate burden after May 1975 when the new legislation came into effect would be between 2.04p and 2.67p in the pound.

Asked by Mr Fiddes if he thought the Council was in a position to borrow £791,260 without excessively affecting the rates, Mr Bigg replied: "If the trend of rising rate values continues to be buoyant, that is my opinion."

Cross-examined by Mr MacDonald, the Chamberlain denied that in the event of borrowing consent being refused a surcharge would be levied on Inverness Town Councillors because they had gone ahead without the Scottish Secretary's approval. He said it could happen only if the Council exceeded the statutory 2.5p on the rates.

'It fell to me to show that the Council's decision was not taken recklessly and that the Council had good grounds for believing they could undertake the project within the financial limits available to them," Mr Bigg recalled in 2001. "I found it exhilarating as I realised I was making my points."

The Council's theatre consultant, John Wyckham, told the Inquiry that at £1,300,00, the Council was getting a bargain. Eden Court would cost £232 per square metre compared with smaller theatres elsewhere which would cost £274 and £306 per square metre. He also reported that the Scottish Film Council was interested in using the facility as a regional film theatre and reminded the Reporter that the building would have many other uses, not just opera and drama but as a venue for more popular entertainment.

Mr Alex Clark, Scottish Secretary of the Association of Theatre Unions and a member of the Scottish Trades Union Congress said the STUC was in favour of Eden Court and considered it would be criminal if it was delayed or abandoned because of the present financial position. "Scotland has enough follies without a half-finished theatre on the banks of the Ness," he declared.

The former chairman of the Highland Area of the Scottish Community Drama Association, Mr Lindsay Hamilton, said the theatre would be a boon to amateur companies and could host the Scottish Finals of the SCDA Festival and the outspoken film and TV actor Robert Urquhart, who owned a hotel at Ullapool, said the theatre's value to the community could not be calculated in financial terms and it was shameful that an Inquiry had to be held.

Stuart Edmond, the deputy secretary of the Highlands and Islands Development Board confirmed the Board, which had already contributed £125,000 to the project, wished it to proceed.

Like Mr Bigg, Provost Smith gave evidence for two hours and denied Mr MacDonald's opening assertion that the Council had refused to publish facts and figures relating to Eden Court. There had been no secrecy, he maintained. Only matters of commercial confidentiality had been discussed in private and statements were subsequently issued to the press and published.

Under cross-examination, the Provost admitted that he had been horrified at the increase in cost but tenders had been accepted on a fixed price basis to ensure the same situation did not arise again and become a burden on the rates.

Asked why the Council proceeded in the face of rising costs and Scottish Office advice, the Provost said the only alternative was to scale down the building which would have caused further delays, not saved any money and not met the growing needs of the area. The Scottish Secretary's predecessor had been advised accordingly.

Sir Donald Cameron of Lochiel, vice-convener of Inverness County Council, said its planning, education and finance committees had agreed to donate £30,000 to the Eden Court Appeal before the higher costs were known, and believed the theatre would be an immense asset to the whole region.

The administrator of the National Theatre, London, Mr A J Easterbrook, rejected any suggestion that the Eden Court plan was over-ambitious. It was the ideal size for the area, he said, neither too small nor too large. It would not be a museum for the classics but could be put to a variety of uses and he was sure it would be a success. The Reporter was told that Eden Court also had the support of the Scottish Arts Council, Scottish Opera and the D'Oyly Carte Opera Company.

Burgh Architect and Town Planning Officer William Jack said Eden Court had not affected the Council's house building or maintenance programmes and he pointed out that the Council was obliged to provide amenities for its tenants. Cross-examined by Mr Fiddes, Mr Jack said there were 1600 on the Council housing waiting list and 56 houses had been built so far that year. A further 1070 were under construction and Eden Court was having no effect on their progress

Giving evidence on behalf of Mr MacDonald, Councillor James Cameron said he had reservations about Eden Court when it was first proposed and thought the money could be used to better purpose. He agreed the town needed a theatre but not of such size and cost. His efforts to have the project abandoned had been unsuccessful. An official visit to Nottingham's civic theatre had confirmed his opinion that the annual deficit on Eden Court could be £200,000 a year.

Mr MacQueen told the Inquiry his objections were on religious, moral and financial grounds and on the council's neglect of more urgent matters. He repeated his by now famous assertion that the theatre was a "house of vanity" and that it was sinful to use consecrated ground for that purpose. It had no virtue and would cater for lusts of the eye and the flesh. Theatre had never prospered in Inverness because the people had always been ruled by the Word of God.

Above
A persistent critic of the spiralling cost of Eden Court, Dalneigh's Labour councillor James Cameron gave evidence against the Town Council at the public inquiry.

His bank manager had advised him that charges on an £800,000 loan would amount to £118,000 a year and to ask the public to bear that burden for a building that would never pay its way was a completely wrong application of public funds and a negation of thrift. The Council should concentrate instead of developing gap sites in the town. He told the Inquiry he was amazed how many people were opposed to the theatre and thought the Council should have other priorities.

Appearing on behalf of Mr MacQueen, the Council's retired Sanitary Inspector John Porteous, said the money would be better employed improving Council houses. Out of more than 3000 he had inspected, only 72 had been upgraded and, as far as he knew, nothing had yet been done to the others.

Mr MacDonald, who objected on grounds of amenity and expense, described Eden Court as a useless prestige project. None of the Council's witnesses had proved it would produce anything other than a large deficit.

It was surprising that in view of the great public support claimed for it, only 342 individuals had responded to the public appeal, he added. Half the money raised had come from local authorities and could not be regarded as coming from the general public. He accused the Council of a lack of openness and a failure to consult residents in the area. He had not been given sight of a consultant's report until the Inquiry started.

Stressing that he was no Philistine and not opposed to theatre, he added: "I believe the Town Council should not have gone ahead with this project on the grounds of cost" and said he had a petition supporting his views.

Summing up, Mr Morrison said evidence that the theatre represented value for money had not been challenged by any qualified person. There was no evidence that it was diverting funds or labour from other Council building work. The Scottish Secretary had previously approved borrowing consent and, as the increase in cost was entirely due to inflation, it would be strange if borrowing consent was not extended.

He appreciated the sincerity of Mr MacQeen's religious views but neither he nor Mr MacDonald had produced any expert evidence to support their arguments. The Council had done so – and the HIDB, the SAC, the STUC and other local authorities supported them. The objectors' case was very meagre and the weight of their objections was light, he maintained.

In his summing up, Mr Fiddes said it was an unpropitious time for the Council to proceed with this project. Costs were rising and the country was facing its most serious economic crisis since the 1930s. Going to the theatre was one of the things the man in the street could do without. Inverness had no theatre-going tradition and Eden Court would have to create one from scratch, attracting people from up to 50 miles away in all kinds of weather.

The case for the theatre was based on assumptions, he went on. It was an act of faith and no one could tell what the effect on the rates would be. It was a status symbol and the Council had persevered with it against the advice of the Secretary Of State and, having spent £600,000, the Council assumed he would give them consent to borrow the rest. "The only practicable alternative might be to close the project down and to hope for better days," he declared.

Two weeks after the Inquiry, in its final budget, the Town Council raised rates by 8.5p – but Treasurer William Fraser announced that Eden Court accounted for only 0.2p of the increase.

In October, the BBC opened a studio and a satellite station, Radio Highland, in Inverness. In the General Election, Labour was re-elected with a majority of three – but the strikes and the three-day week continued. Even the Northern Institute For the Blind was affected. It reported that inflation had caused its deficit to soar from £300 to £4000. In its leader of 11th November, the Courier commented that the government's first budget did not seem to do much for the country's economic ills and that the financial outlook remained gloomy.

The Inverness Arts Guild programme continued. The Florians sparkled in a Noel Coward comedy and the Council banned "The Exorcist" from the La Scala. One supporter of the decision described the film as "blasphemous and harrowing". The chart-topping pop group The Tremeloes appeared in the Caledonian Ballroom.

Noting that work on Eden Court was continuing, Mr MacQueen wrote to the Courier on 19th November: "We should be encouraged by the fact that it is written: 'The desire of the wicked shall perish'. Psalm 112 v10."

In the same issue, the Courier carried a letter from Frederic Lloyd, general manager of D'Oyly Carte, qualifying the company's reported support for Eden Court. "In these days, with Inverness developing as it is, it would have been invaluable if the Council had built the theatre on the lines of many Scandinavian theatres to seat up to 1200 people for

Above and below
Eden Court construction

Above
Another graduate of Inverness Royal Academy music productions Janis Kelly, who went on to win acclaim with the English National Opera and Opera Factory, returned to Eden Court in Scottish Opera's "Die Fledermaus".

opera, ballet and musical performances but to close it down to almost half that capacity for other entertainments." he commented. "It does mean that visiting companies of any size from the south will be dependent entirely on guarantees which must necessarily be paid by the local authority."

By coincidence, Inverness Opera Company was presenting a Gilbert & Sullivan evening in the Town Hall later that month and Inverness Royal Academy staged "The Gondoliers" with Jimmy Chisholm, Gordon Tocher and Peter Kelly in the cast. Chisholm went on to become a professional actor and would appear several times at Eden Court. Janis Kelly was the soprano soloist in Inverness Choral Society's performance of Fauré's "Requiem". Britain's leading oboe soloist, Evelyn Barbirolli, appeared for Inverness Music Society.

Teachers and busmen joined the hauliers on strike – but the news was not all gloomy, however. Inverness entered the jet age with a strengthened and lengthened runway at Dalcross airport and the chairman of the HIDB's consultative council, the eminent High Court judge Lord Cameron, said the Highlands was on the threshold of a new era. The chance for economic, educational and social development had to be grasped and used wisely, he declared. Warning against pinning too many hopes on North Sea Oil developments, he said basic industries like fishing, farming and handicrafts would form the foundation for a prosperous and well-balanced future with Inverness Technical College offering the potential to meet expanding needs.

Reflecting the law lord's comments, the town's artistic life continued to flourish. In February, the Scottish Baroque Ensemble gave a concert in the Caledonian Ballroom, Martin Carthy played at the Folk Club in the Albert Hotel and a fiddle festival was held in the unsuitable surroundings of Rose Street Hall which was also pressed into service for the Lindsay String Quartet when the Little Theatre was otherwise engaged. Janis Kelly returned with Harry Nicoll to sing Haydn's "Creation" with Inverness Choral Society and Scots poet Norman McCaig and the star of TV's "Steptoe & Son", Harry H. Corbett, appeared at the Town Hall – but not together.

Part of Inverness High Street was proposed for commercial redevelopment, Marks & Spencer were said to be coming to the new Eastgate shopping centre, another indoor sports centre was proposed for the Bught Park, a new police HQ was opened and Scottish Secretary Willie Ross inaugurated the new Hydro Electric scheme at Foyers.

NORIKO OHARA *SCOTTISH BALLET*

Above
Inverness Opera Company pose for a picture prior to their 1984 Eden Court performance of "The Merry Widow".

" ...I always enjoy going to Inverness. Everything is fantastic...backstage, the restaurant ...and the setting is so lovely..."

"I danced on opening night and was amazed when I saw the theatre. All the other Scottish theatres I performed in were traditional. I can't remember how many times I have danced at Eden Court since. I did 'Swan Lake', 'Romeo & Juliet', 'Anna Karenina'... and when we did 'Nutcracker' in 1979 we had to cancel because of the snow. The stage floor is a bit noisy – it's like iron – but I always enjoy going to Inverness. Everything is fantastic… backstage, the restaurant … and the setting is so lovely."

In March, The Scottish Arts Council's budget was increased by 26% to £3,000,000 and director Sandy Dunbar promised Eden Court its share of the largesse. Work on the theatre was proceeding although the Council was still waiting to hear the outcome of the public inquiry and Provost Smith had undertaken to tackle the Scottish Secretary when he met him at Foyers.

A week before the Scottish Secretary's visit, however, it was announced that borrowing consent of £791,000 had been granted and, at a ceremony in the Provost's room on 28th March 1975, the Highland Board handed over its cheque for £150,000. It was, Provost Smith declared, a heart-warming week for those who had devoted years of planning and work to the project.

The Council's actions, it seemed, had been vindicated.

CHAPTER FIVE

"A VICTORY FOR COMMON SENSE"

On 15th April, 1975, Eden Court's Board Of Governors announced that it had appointed Murray Edwards to be director of the new theatre. A chemistry graduate of Edinburgh University where he had been a member of the dramatic society and organised three Highland tours, he had been awarded a Scottish Arts Council bursary to study theatre administration and after two years as publicity manager at the Octagon Theatre, Bolton, he had been appointed general manager of the Thorndyke Theatre in Leatherhead, Surrey, a new theatre similar in size and function to Eden Court.

Mr Edwards had not been the Board's first choice, however. It had offered the post to an older and apparently more experienced man, Reginald Birks from Hertfordshire. He declined the appointment, but it was not the last the Board had heard from Mr Birks. He re-applied for the job three years later when Edwards left – but did not make the short list.

Equity's Scottish organiser, Alex Clark, who had given evidence on the Council's behalf at the previous year's inquiry visited Inverness that Spring and urged trade unionists to become involved in Eden Court, ensuring its fullest multi-purpose use, particularly among young people, and developing attitudes to the arts lacking in other parts of Scotland.

Opportunities were already available. The New England Repertory Company visited the Little Theatre to stage the Neil Simon comedy, "Come Blow Your Horn", Inverness Opera Company used the same venue for "The Boy Friend" and was followed by The Margaret Firth School Of Dancing's annual "Merry-Go-Round". Russell Hunter returned to Inverness with a new one-man show celebrating another Scottish historical figure, "Knox".

Inverness Town Council held its "greeting meeting" and tributes were paid to Provost Smith who although elected to the new District Council had not stood as Provost. Presenting his closing statement, Treasurer W A E Fraser said he was handing over to the new district authority a burgh, which, despite inflation and thanks to careful spending, was the lowest-rated burgh in Scotland.

On 23rd June, Douglas Baxter died in the Royal Northern Infirmary. He was 61. "Douglas didn't talk a lot about the meetings but I know there were terrible differences of opinion," his widow commented. "I could see he was under terrible strain and, quite honestly, I think that caused the cancer."

Left
A party of Inverness Town Councillors, including leading opponent Dan Corbett (left), are shown progress on building the interior of Eden Court.

Below
Trying to reconcile expectations and financial reality – Murray Edwards (right), the first director of Eden Court Theatre.

Above
Robert Fasken, secretary and later member of the Highlands & Islands Development Board, became the agency's representative on Eden Court's Board Of Governors and a champion of the theatre.

Educated in Glasgow, he had worked as a shipbroker and social worker before graduating from Glasgow University with an arts degree. He later entered the Church of Scotland ministry and served as Scots chaplain to the forces in Hong Kong before moving to the Highlands, serving on Lochaber District Council and Sutherland Education Committee. He eventually settled in Inverness and was elected to the Town Council in 1965, serving as Dean Of Guild, bailie and chairman of the Planning Committee. After retiring from the Council, he became chairman of the Eden Court Management Committee, a vacancy that was to be filled by his deputy, Peter Donald.

With a lifelong interest in the arts, Rev. Baxter vigorously championed the cause of Eden Court and although he died before it could be completed, he had the satisfaction of knowing that a major financial obstacle had been cleared and that his dream was fast becoming reality.

The transition to the new local government structure was accomplished smoothly with Provost Iain Fraser becoming chief advocate for Eden Court. Inverness District Council, feeling unable to absorb the cost of the theatre's £800,000 loan on its rates and recognising that the building would serve the entire region, asked Highland Region to assume ownership and take over the interest charges, estimated at £92,000 a year.

In August 1975, the Region's Leisure & Recreation Committee under the chairmanship of the late Councillor William Swanson, Thurso, who is commemorated in the name of the town's art gallery, agreed to the Council's request but decided not to contribute to any deficit on the theatre's first year running costs, estimated at £70,000. The Scottish Arts Council, it was told, would be contributing £30,000 and the balance would remain the District's responsibility.

"I am still of the opinion that we are being generous and considerate in meeting the capital cost charges and saying we would consider from year to year any contribution we could make to the running costs of the theatre," commented Rev Nicolson, the Council Convener.

The developments did not attract any public comment from Mr MacQueen or Mr MacDonald. The former was not silent, however. He was now writing to the Courier about inflation.

At the end of August, the Phoenix Drama Club staged "Doctor In The House" at the Little Theatre; the recently-established Inverness Film Society began a new season at the same venue the following month and Inverness Strathspey & Reel Society made their first recording under the leadership of Donald Riddell.

In October, the Scottish Secretary approved the massive housing development at Smithton, Culloden and Balloch.

Below
The construction of the new theatre in progress

Inverness was growing faster than many people appreciated or expected and the local authorities were keeping pace.

Changes were imminent at the Highland Board too. Professor Kenneth Alexander was appointed to succeed Sir Andrew Gilchrist as chairman and Robert Fasken was appointed to the Board. Iain MacAskill succeeded him as Board Secretary.

Two brochures were published, promoting the range of performances to be staged at Eden Court and its conference facilities. A permanent fund-raising organisation, The Friends Of Eden Court, was also launched that month offering talks, meet-the-artist opportunities, social events, priority booking and ticket concessions as membership incentives.

The comedy duo, Hinge & Bracket, and The Boys Of The Lough appeared at the Town House and the leading British Country & Western band, The Hillsiders, were booked by the newly-formed Inverness Country & Western Club which held its performances at the Coach-house Inn, Stoneyfield.

At its meeting on Monday 20th October, Inverness District Council was told that Eden Court would open on 15th April and it was agreed full-time appointments would be considered in January. It was also announced that The Northern Meeting would hold the first ball on the fully-extended stage floor.

The increase in the estimated cost of the theatre had not ended with the Public Inquiry, however. At the end of October the Highland Regional Council's Leisure & Recreation Committee was told that the price had risen by a further £454,940, bringing the total estimated cost to almost £1.8 million.

In a report to the committee, the District Council's chief executive, Ian Miller, former clerk to Ross & Cromarty County Council and thereby widely known and respected by many of Ross-shire's regional councillors, said 75% of the increase could be attributed to an increase in the main contractor's costs, £69,000 in consequential fees and £51,000 to equipping and furnishing the theatre. Loan charges on the additional cost would amount to a further £86,100.

A letter from the theatre's management committee stressed that they were not responsible for the increase in construction costs. Their remit was in preparing the theatre, appointing staff, budgeting for the running costs and planning the programme in association with the director.

Unlike the Region, the ever-nervous District – as so often before – had earlier considered the latest increase in private and not issued a statement to the press.

Left
As the first chairman, businessman Edwin Robertson set the agenda for The Friends Of Eden Court's wide range of fund-raising activities.

However, the decision to open the theatre on a Sunday for the screening of films was not considered sufficiently confidential or controversial to warrant private discussion, although the open debate did reveal opposition. Theatre director Murray Edwards said the move had been taken into account in the budget and that the films would not be the type normally shown by commercial cinemas. They would be chosen by a committee in association with the Scottish Film Council whose support for Eden Court had been conditional on the screening of 70 films a year. The Courier reporter noted: "After further discussion during which some members showed a tendency to moralise or sermonise instead of getting down to basic facts, the Council approved Sunday films by 15 votes to seven."

On Sunday 2nd November, Eden Court lost its second champion when Ex-Provost Smith died in the Royal Northern Infirmary at the age of 76. He had joined the Town Council in

Right
Site quantity surveyor Derek Gardiner, later chairman of Friends of Eden Court and a producer of the Scout Gang Show staged at Eden Court.

1961 and served three terms as Provost. The Courier obituary noted: "He was steadfast in his support of Eden Court for which he and many former town councillors had been striving since 1967 and in whose opening next year he would have taken such pride and pleasure.

"He maintained, sometimes against strong opposition, that a rapidly developing and important town like Inverness urgently required such a project and he stuck to his guns when the estimated cost began to rise and a public inquiry was held. Eden Court was a development which would be of benefit not only to Inverness but to a large part of the Highlands, he said, and one day they would be proud of it."

Two days before being re-admitted to the RNI for a serious operation, the newspaper obituary added, ex-Provost Smith had attended a Council meeting about the theatre. Describing him as "a history maker" and the leader of the Eden Court campaign, the Courier's leader commented: "It is sad he did not live to see it open and in use. Even those who, like ourselves, still consider the project ill-advised, ill-timed and too costly, could not fail to appreciate the efforts he put in to see his dream become reality."

The theatre's capacity to generate strong feelings, even beyond the boundaries of Inverness, had not diminished. That month, the chairman of Nairn Tourist Association, Arthur Marshall, resigned in protest at Nairn District Council's decision to donate £1000 to Eden Court. A former town councillor, he told the Nairnshire Telegraph the money could have been better spent on amenities in the town.

On Monday 24th November, Inverness District Council went into private again – despite efforts by councillors Ron Lyon and Dan Corbett. Councillor Lyon claimed all discussion about Eden Court was now in private and the Council had reached the stage where they were confusing controversiality with confidentiality. "It's high time discussions were out in the open and people really knew what was happening," he declared.

Councillor Corbett reminded Provost Iain Fraser he had advocated more open-ness about Eden Court and was told the Provost had not changed his views but extremely delicate circumstances justified this matter being considered in private at present.

A press statement was later issued and disclosed that an application for further consent to borrow a further £411,000 had been made in August – and that the Scottish Office had summoned Council representatives and their consultants to a meeting in Edinburgh.

Five days after a public meeting in the former Mercury Hotel had formally constituted The Friends Of Eden Court under the enterprising chairmanship of Inverness businessman Edwin Robertson, it was announced that the District Council planned to hold a public meeting outlining the reasons for seeking additional borrowing consent of £411,000. Councillors, consultants and representatives of the Highland Board and Scottish Arts Council would be in attendance.

On Wednesday 3rd December, a special meeting of the Council was told that the £411,000 for which borrowing consent was being sought had already been spent on Eden Court and members agreed the Chief Executive should meet Scottish Office officials in Edinburgh and explain the reasons for the latest increase in Eden Court's estimated cost. The final cost was expected to be known the following week, it was reported.

Councillors demanded to know how the cost of a fixed price contract could increase and consultant quantity surveyor James Jaffrey said he could not understand how they had got the idea that the contract had a fixed price.

"I have never used the term 'fixed price contract'," he declared. "The only way to get a fixed price contract is on a small job. It would never work on a sophisticated project such as the one we have." Asked why the Council had not been told it was not a fixed price contract, Mr Jaffrey said: "Perhaps because everyone understood it wasn't."

Project architect Graham Law said the main cost of the increase was due to the bankruptcy of the steel sub-contracting firm at a time when steel was unavailable. The subsequent delay in appointing another sub-contractor and obtaining steel disrupted a carefully-calculated programme and, as a result, compensation had to be paid to the other companies involved in the Eden Court contract. Of the 30 firms approached, only one tendered for the steel sub-contract and its price had to be accepted if further delays were not to be incurred, Mr Law added.

Asked if someone had failed to notify the Council that £1.3m was no longer the "ceiling price", Mr Wyckham said it hadn't been him. "It was impossible to foresee that a reputable 100-year-old steel firm would go bankrupt," he stated.

In 2001, site quantity surveyor Derek Gardiner could still recall the atmosphere at that meeting. "It was nasty," he commented. "When the meeting finally went into private, the councillor who had been leading the attack fell asleep and things calmed down – but I was appalled. It gave me an insight into the attitude among certain councillors towards Eden Court.

"But they wouldn't have had the experience to know there was no such thing as a fixed price contract in the industry or why things could happen to add to the price.

"The normal conditions of contracts used at that time on practically every contract – and certainly for every local authority contract – was the standard form of building contract under which the contractor had priced bills of quantity and fills out a tender. But there are conditions under the terms of the contract where that can be varied, particularly where there are delays caused by the employer or their agents, the contractor and, shall we say, an act of God.

"The biggest thing that caused the cost of the contract to go up was the nominated steel contractor going into liquidation just before the steel was required which was immediately before the three-day week started – and at that time the building industry was absolutely booming. All the order books were full and builders and contractors had so much work they could almost name their price.

"Because it was the architect's duty to nominate the sub-contractors and that represented a delay caused by the employer's agents which extended the construction period, it meant the contractor was entitled to reimbursement," he explained. "Steel was desperately scarce and firms wouldn't price. They had a lot of work already and weren't interested. That meant going abroad before eventually finding a firm just outside Warwick that could do it. That all took time in which the roof and floor couldn't be built because it needed steel."

Above
The chapel of the Bishop's Palace became the performers' Green Room.

"WHAT EDEN COURT COURT MEANS TO ME"

CALUM MACDONALD RUNRIG

"...it's always good to go back. It's a special place for us."

"Until we played Eden Court, we'd been a dance band playing in village halls. Appearing at the theatre was the first time we put on a proper concert of our own material. We put a lot of money and effort into it, we even put up the posters ourselves. It was a big risk for us because we didn't know what the response was going to be – but it was a sell-out and that gave us the confidence to go on and do more concerts elsewhere. For many years we didn't play Eden Court but it's always good to go back. It's a special place for us."

"The new sub-contractor named his price and had to go to Germany to get his steel and this all added to the delay," Mr Gardiner continued. "There wasn't a complete stoppage of work but the whole job had to be slowed down and was put out of sequence for about four months – and the contractor was entitled to be paid for that time. There was nothing abnormal about that. Crudens co-operated all the way. They were tough but they never got nasty.

"Moreover, the contract was pushed forward into a period of increased labour and material costs no-one could have anticipated at the time the contract was signed. There was also the asbestos scare and, as the steel beams were to be sprayed with asbestos, the standard precaution against fire until that time, a new material had to be found and it inevitably cost extra. That again was no fault of the contractor. We also found a lot of dry rot in the Bishop's Palace which had to be eradicated and that added to the final price."

When he came to Inverness in 1959, Mr Gardiner had cause to look at the newspaper files for reports on the opening of the municipal swimming baths in the '30s. "Exactly the same thing happened then as happened over Eden Court... a local authority project, delays, increased costs, public controversy," he revealed. "Yet, by the time Eden Court was being built, how many people passed the swimming pool and said 'That should never have been built; look what it cost'? And nobody says that about Eden Court today. Looking back, it was absolutely worth it."

"By the time the steel contractor went bust, the building was well under construction and we had no choice but to proceed and seek additional borrowing consent," ex-Provost William Fraser added.

Even at £1.9million, John Wyckham remains convinced the Council got a bargain. Semi-retired in 2001, he said: "The price may have seemed daunting in the mid '70s but if you look at that sort of building today, it would cost £8.5 million."

Although the theatre's latest financial crisis had triggered anger and recrimination within the Council Chamber, outside Inverness's artistic life continued apace with the Alberni String Quartet at the Little Theatre and Inverness Choral Society's Christmas Concert at St Columba's – but on Monday 15th December there were further financial shocks in store for the Council when it was told that the revenue budget for Eden Court's first year of operation showed an estimated deficit of almost £250,000.

Theatre director Murray Edwards said additional staff were required for the theatre and that had contributed to the increase in estimated expenditure. The theatre's management committee couldn't disclaim responsibility for this discrepancy and it was agreed that the Provost, Council vice-chairman Hamish Bauchop and Leisure & Recreation Committee chairman Allan Sellar should be added to the management committee to strengthen the Council's voice and that, in future, its meetings be held in public.

It also agreed to abandon Phase II of the project, which included a studio theatre, workshop and scene dock and was costed at £50,000.

The Courier leader on 19th December branded Eden Court as "the Highlands' biggest white elephant". "Presumably because the building is so far advanced and to call a halt would be stupid, permission for borrowing consent will be forthcoming since we do not think the European Economic Community would look very kindly on a request for assistance for a project that should never have been started, should have been costed properly and, if it was costed properly, there should have been a full awareness of the 'small type' to be found in most contracts relating to the increase in wages, supplies etc," wrote Miss Barron, by now the project's sternest and most stentorian critic.

Three days later, Inverness District Council was told there was every chance they would be given Scottish Office approval to borrow an additional £200,000 for Eden Court. Mr Miller, the Council's Finance Director Alan Imlah and the theatre consultants had met Scottish Office officials and explained the reasons for the increase in costs, which would now amount to a final total of £1,950,255. A final decision would be made as a matter of urgency.

The Council agreed to discuss the future funding and management of the theatre with the Highland Board. It also considered a full breakdown of the theatre's 1976/77 running costs, which revealed staff salaries amounted to £61,221, overheads to £260,000 and artists's fees to £182,100. Box Office income was estimated at £203,766, with grants from the Scottish Arts Council of £40,000 and from the Scottish Film Council of £1000, creating an apparent deficit of around £250,000.

The Courier hit out again but a note of reality and acceptance had crept into the leader. "White elephant though it is, it is unfortunately in our midst and leaving it standing there unfitted-out and empty would make it even more of a burden upon the community so there would be no

Right
One of Inverness's most gifted amateur actors whose son went on to star in STV's "High Road" and many major stage productions, Jimmy Chisholm Snr. rehearses a scene from The Phoenix Theatre Group's 1966 production of "Antigone".

chance of any income to offset some of the expenditure," it read. "Moreover, it is hardly likely ever to pay its way and it may as well be given a chance to try and make its losses as low as possible, the initial mistake on the former Town Council's part being to embark upon such an unnecessarily ambitious project."

Meanwhile, Eden Court's director, Mr Murray Edwards was busy compensating for the Council's lack of public relations skills by undertaking a series of promotional engagements.

On 14th January 1976, he addressed the Inverness University Women's Association and gave an interview to the Evening Express in which he pledged that Eden Court would cater for the tastes of young people by booking pop groups like the currently popular Bay City Rollers a Scottish band catering for the younger and perhaps less discerning end of the teen market.

And so a momentous year drew to a close with Santa Claus calling early at Inverness Town House and the season of goodwill apparently affecting Eden Court's most persistent opponents. With the theatre nearing completion, they were albeit somewhat reluctantly beginning to bow to reality – but in the New Year the Council's resolution and nerve was to be severely tested yet again.

EDEN COURT THEATRE
was opened at a ceremony
performed on Thursday 15th April 1976
by Andrew Cruickshank M.B.E.

CHAPTER SIX

CURTAIN UP!

Further confirmation that the Council was not pursuing Eden Court to the exclusion of other amenities for the town came on 15th January 1976 when it agreed to explore the possibility of building an indoor sports centre at the Bught Park.

With Scots singer Peter Morrison due to give a concert in the Town House, the Council's Policy & Resources Committee learned on Monday 20th January that Eden Court was not eligible for a grant from the European Regional Development Fund – but the Scottish Office confirmed that, pending a full examination of the Council's case, it was to grant provisional consent for borrowing £150,000 to meet the Council's immediate commitments to Eden Court.

"You will appreciate that the further escalation of cost to a total somewhere in the region of £1.95m gives cause for grave concern," the department's letter read. "I must stress that this consent is given without prejudice to a decision on giving further consent to incur further capital expenditure. Such a decision must wait the completion of our inquiries. In the meantime I would be obliged if you would inform me as soon as possible of the total cost of the project and of the exact amount of capital expenditure for which consent may now be sought."

Appalled at the prospect of The Bay City Rollers appearing at Eden Court, older teenagers wrote to the Courier appealing to the theatre's director to book other bands instead and warning that the notoriously demonstrative Rollers fans – who had hitherto revealed a capacity for doing little more than waving tartan scarves above their heads – would tear the new theatre apart.

Another letter called on Mr Edwards to ensure that Country & Western artists were well represented in the theatre's programme and citing a list for his consideration. The correspondent wrote back the following week withdrawing the name of Patsy Cline – as it had been pointed out to him that she was dead.

Mr MacQueen returned to the fray deploring the increase in the "cruel costs" of Eden Court at a time of deepening recession and calling for no contribution to be made from the town's Common Good Fund towards reducing what he described as the practically insatiable debt for an unsustainable folly requiring a loan of £1,202,260.

At the end of the month, District and Regional representatives met to discuss financial responsibility for the project and the working party agreed to recommend that the region assume ownership of Eden Court and pay the loan's annual interest of £175,000.

Not unexpectedly, Provost Iain Fraser described the outcome as very satisfactory and hoped the Council would accept – but the chairman of the District's Finance Committee, Councillor William Fraser, the former Burgh Treasurer, was concerned that townspeople who had contributed to the Eden Court Appeal might object to the District relinquishing ownership of the theatre.

Councillor Peter Drummond, a member of the theatre's management committee, expressed reluctance but was concerned at the consequences of the Council bearing the loan charges. It would not be easy to get regional agreement, he predicted.

On Wednesday 4th February, however, the Region's Leisure & Recreation Committee decided to recommend to the full council that, subject to the District receiving borrowing consent from the Scottish Office, it should take over Eden Court and its loan charges, leasing it back to the District to operate and pay the running costs. The effect of the decision

Left
Scottish stage and screen actor Andrew Cruickshank (centre), a star of TV's popular "Dr Finlay's Casebook", unveils the plaque commemorating his opening of the theatre. Also in the picture, Provost Ian Fraser (left), and Peter Donald.

Right
Invergordon councillor Isobel Rhind, convener of the Highland Region's Social Work Committee and later a theatre governor, protested at paying more for Eden Court and less on caring for children, the infirm and the elderly.

local authority spending, recalling the limited amounts that her committee had earlier agreed to spend on children's homes, home helps and care for the elderly.

"I can't see any justification for the placing of this burden on my ratepayers," declared Glencoe councillor Major Eric Moss and Durness councillor Francis Keith, the Planning Committee chairman, said he had to think of the people of North West Sutherland who would never use Eden Court and would resent their money being spent on it.

Council convener Murdo Nicolson swayed the meeting when he reminded the committee that the Council had accepted liabilities inherited from other parts of the region. "It is unfair to wipe our hands and leave it to the District," he declared. "We should make some contribution to support this project which could become our prize possession."

The decision was endorsed by the Council's Policy & Resources Committee on Wednesday 18th February when it was revealed that Regional rates could rise by 30p in the £ because of government cuts in its Rate Support Grant.

"There is a growing feeling that frills should wait upon better days and undoubtedly there is going to be considerably more heat generated over the cost to the public of Eden Court," the Courier leader commented. "That cost, moreover, includes loan charges as well as running costs and it is disturbing, rightly, some of the further-flung parts of Highland Region to be rated in support of this white elephant. On the other hand, it has often disturbed the more urban areas to be rated more highly for helping to provide a wide variety of services to the 'outposts'."

Backing was also forthcoming from the Region's Finance Committee where, revealing a change of heart and mind, the motion was moved by Major Moss. "My area won't benefit much but we must face facts that the building is there and we won't get rid of it," he said. "It would be impossible for Inverness District Council to face the cost alone."

Inverness councillor Peter Drummond agreed. The District had possibly over-stretched itself, he said, but its ratepayers contributed to projects in other areas and it was not unreasonable for other areas to reciprocate.

What mattered now, the Courier maintained in its leader of 20th February, was that the theatre be used to the full to support its running costs and keep the rate burden to a minimum.

Advertisements in the same issue of the newspaper reveal that a two-bedroomed detached house cost £12,000 at that

on the Region's rates would be 1.25p in the £; if it remained in District ownership, it would add 4.5p in the £ to the District rate, the committee was told.

Powerful opposition was ranged against the recommendation. Councillor John Robertson, chairman of the Region's Finance Committee, said the sum was twice that which the Leisure & Recreation Committee had just agreed to spend on library books and Invergordon councillor Isobel Rhind, chairman of Highland Region's Social Work Committee, said the Region had to consider its own priorities. She reminded her colleagues of the government's anti-inflation policy and the guidelines it had imposed on time and technical and clerical staff at Eden Court were being sought at salaries of £2000 a year.

TIE-Up Theatre, a local company formed by drama graduate John Doyle who had appeared in Inverness Royal Academy productions, had set up in the town and staged a pantomime at The Little Theatre that did not attract big audiences. A Courier correspondent commented that did not augur well for Eden Court, and, in the continuing absence of a suitable venue in Inverness, Scottish Opera announced that it was taking a full production of Mozart's "Don Giovanni" to Elgin Town Hall in March.

A minor milestone occurred on Thursday 6th February and reminded the public that the day was not far off when Scottish Opera would be staging full-scale productions in Inverness. Eden Court's management committee met in the Bishop's Palace – now part of the new complex – for the first time. It agreed to offer reductions to school parties to encourage young people to discover the benefits of going to the theatre.

The following Wednesday, representatives of the Press were shown round the complex by Eden Court's newly-appointed public relations officer, David Carruthers, who had trained as an actor and appeared in a TV play directed by Ken Loach. The Press declared themselves suitably impressed with the facilities.

The Corries were returning to Inverness to play at the High School Hall, an accordion festival and fiddle championship was to be held in the Town Hall and Anne Lorne Gillies and Glasgow comedian Larry Marshall were appearing at the Caledonian Ballroom. Calum Kennedy, daughter Fiona and comedian Johnny Beattie were also Caley-bound and Inverness Opera Company was to stage the hit musical "Cabaret" in the Inverness Royal Academy hall.

At a press conference in the Town Hose on Wednesday 25th February, Provost Fraser announced that the veteran Scots actor Andrew Cruickshank, best-known for his performance of Dr Cameron in the BBC TV series "Dr Finlay's Casebook", had been invited to perform the official opening ceremony at Eden Court on 15th April.

"Douglas had wanted Yehudi Menuhin to open it - but he wasn't available," ex-Councillor Milne recalled. "Nevertheless, we were delighted to get someone Scottish and as well-known as Andrew Cruickshank. He wouldn't accept a fee; he wanted paid in malt whisky instead."

Above
TIE-Up Theatre Director John Doyle who went on to work at Eden Court, The Swan Theatre, Worcester, and Liverpool's Everyman Theatre.

left
Anne Lorne Gillies who was later to star as 'Mother Goose' at Eden Court.

The gala performance would include the world premiere by the Scottish National Orchestra of a set of symphonic variations specially commissioned for the occasion from composer William Wordsworth who lived in Kincraig and was a descendant of the poet's brother. This William Wordsworth was also a member of Eden Court's new Board Of Governors.

Around 150 official guests – among them ex-Provost W. J. MacKay and the widows of Provost Smith and Councillor Baxter – were to be invited to the opening and an accompanying civic reception. The remaining seats for the performance which would feature excerpts from opera, ballet and drama would be sold to the general public.

On 4th March, Inverness District Councillors breathed a huge sigh of relief when Highland Regional Council agreed to accept Eden Court and its loan charges – although it would have been unprecedented for members to defy recommendations from its Finance and Policy & Resources Committees. Provost Fraser reported the news to the Eden Court board, which met that evening when it was learned that Friends Of Eden Court had already acquired a membership of 464 – one third of it from outwith Inverness.

Above
Inverness MP Russell Johnston backed Council acquisition of the Empire, welcomed the opening of Eden Court and took up the controversy of the "fixed price" contract.

EDEN COURT THEATRE

BOX OFFICE OPENS MONDAY, 22nd MARCH
FOR POSTAL AND TELEPHONE BOOKINGS ONLY

Box Office Telephone Number
Inverness 221718

Priority Bookings for the Friends of Eden Court is Now Open

Dates for your April Diary

THURSDAY, 1st APRIL — 10.00 a.m. BOX OFFICE OPENS FOR COUNTER BOOKINGS. At this time a limited number of seats, price £3 each, for the Opening Gala Performance will be available to the public by **personal application only**. There will be a maximum of 2 seats per applicant.
Our Spacious and Comfortable Restaurant will be Open for Morning Coffee, Lunches, Snacks and Teas.

15th APRIL —
Opening Gala Performance.

16th APRIL —
Inverness 8th Annual Folk Festival.

17th APRIL —
Film Gala Performance "Alice Doesn't Live Here Anymore."

20th-24th APRIL —
"The Country Wife," by William Wycherely.

25th APRIL —
Film : "Day For Night."

26th APRIL —
The Scottish National Orchestra.

27th APRIL —
John Cairney in "The Ivor Novello Show."

28th APRIL —
The McCalmans in Concert.

29th APRIL to 1st MAY —
Scottish Community Drama Association Finals.

For further details of our programme of events, seat prices and concessions, please write to:—
MAILING LIST,
EDEN COURT THEATRE,
Bishops Road, Inverness, IV3 5SA.

Right
Eden Court unveils its opening attractions in a newspaper advertisement.

Inverness's Liberal Member of Parliament, Russell Johnston, welcomed the Highland Council's decision and said he was very happy Eden Court was virtually complete. "I believe it is a most important part of the provision available to a community that there is somewhere where art, culture and entertainment can be presented," he told the Press.

He had misgivings at the cost of the project, maintaining the Council could have acquired and redeveloped the Empire Theatre for much less but he supported the Council wholeheartedly once the decision had been made.

Nevertheless the MP sympathised with critics who complained at the public inquiry of a lack of information about costs, and was concerned about the confusion over what people had been led to believe was a fixed price contract.

Recalling a letter published in the Highland News asking whose job it was to inform the Council and the public that it was not a fixed price contract, he had written to Scottish

Under Secretary Frank McElhone in a bid to settle this unsolved mystery.

Mr McElhone said it was a firm contract, not a fixed one, and saw no reason for any confusion but Mr Johnston was not satisfied and decided to pursue the matter. "However much I and others were anxious to see this project go ahead and be proud that it has been completed, I certainly would not wish this result to have been achieved by false impressions being given at a public inquiry," he declared.

Having received a decision from Highland Regional Council, Inverness District Council was able to finalise its budget and on Monday 8th March approved a rate increase of 2p in the pound – which was less than it would have been if the Council had been left with Eden Court's loan charges.

Although a free public performance was to be held with local artists to test the facilities at Eden Court, the BBC Scotland became the first to use the theatre, filming the TV programme, "Current Account" in the foyer. The discussion about the role and achievements of the Highland Board featured its new chairman, Professor Kenneth Alexander. BBC Radio 2 was also to broadcast the finals of the international Nordring Music Prize which it was to host in the theatre in June.

Booking for the theatre's first season opened on 1st April and demonstrated that Inverness was joining the mainstream of the nation's culture. Apart from the opening gala, forthcoming attractions included an appearance at the 8th Inverness Folk Festival by Ireland's Bothy Band, the first film performance – the Inverness premiere of Martin Scorsese's "Alice Doesn't Live Here Anymore" with an Oscar-winning performance by Ellen Burstyn, classic plays by the Oxford Playhouse and Edinburgh's Royal Lyceum Theatre, concerts by the Scottish National Orchestra and the recently-formed Scottish Chamber Orchestra which would be making its public debut in Inverness, productions of "Giselle" and "Tales Of Hoffman" by Scottish Ballet, "The Merry Widow" and "Confessions Of A Justified Sinner" by Scottish Opera and Eden Court's first pop concert by The Edgar Broughton Band.

Well-known TV actor Gerald Flood was to star in the West End comedy "There's A Girl In My Soup", and popular Scots actor Iain Cuthbertson was to appear with singer Helen MacArthur in a musical travelogue of early 19th century Scotland, "Mr Topham's Diary". Local users would include Inverness Music Festival, the Margaret Firth School Of Dancing and Inverness High School pupils. Tickets cost between 60p and £1.80 with a top price of £4 for the opera.

Right
The distinguished British actor Sir Derek Jacobi – later TV's Claudius and Cadfael – appeared as "Hamlet" at Eden Court's opening gala.

It was also announced that ballet dancer Donald MacLeary, son of an Inverness chemist, was emerging from his recently announced retirement from the Royal Ballet to appear at Eden Court's opening gala when he would partner, prima ballerina Doreen Wells in the balcony pas-de-deux from Prokofiev's "Romeo And Juliet". Now the company's balletmaster, he had often partnered Margot Fonteyn and Svetlana Beriosova at Covent Garden and had danced a leading role in Kenneth MacMillan's ragtime ballet "Elite Syncopations", recently seen on television.

The finals of the Scottish Community Drama Association's Festival Of One-Act Plays would also be staged at Eden Court in April and would be opened by Inverness Florians, who had won through with the play, "Once Upon A Seashore" by

Above
Eden Court - the completed building.

Donald East. Other Highland teams taking part were Rogart Amateur Dramatic Society and Thurso Players.

Meanwhile, the La Scala was screening "Jaws" for the first time and about to go head-to-head with Eden Court's Sunday film shows by screening the first in a series of X-rated films. Carl Dolmetsch gave a recital on period instruments for Inverness Music Society and Tie-Up staged "The Glass Menagerie" by Tennessee Wlliams at The Little Theatre.

Having already attracted the disapproval from some religious quarters, the theatre's management committee was anxious that the theatre should have some church use and the Church Of Scotland was to hold a service of Praise in the theatre on Sunday 25th April led by thirteen local choirs directed by Norman Cairns, Dingwall.

The Courier marked the countdown to opening day with a leader "Unrepentantly, we maintain our view that something smaller, less grandiose, less expensive and less ambitious is all that is needed, for the occasions which are most likely to fill or nearly fill the 800 seats are few in number," it read. "Naturally, it will please every ratepayer even more than audiences if we prove false prophets but, in these inflationary days, expensive seat prices to attract audiences are not likely to go all that far in meeting costs."

It also pointed out that seven-day running was considered essential to maximise revenue but there were no Monday performances in the first three months of operation. "They may be used for dress rehearsals but it does weaken the argument for Sunday opening."

Miss Barron was perhaps unaware that Mondays were to be used as "get-in" day for companies staging a week's run at the theatre and in the 17th April issue, carrying a full report of the theatre's opening and gala concert, the leader asked what Bishop Eden and his successors in the palace – whose denomination observed the occasion more fully than other Scottish churches – would have made of opening Eden Court in Holy Week. The answer was given some weeks later when the Representative Church Council of the Scottish

Episcopalian Church blessed Eden Court with its annual conference, addressed by the Archbishop Of Canterbury, Dr Donald Coggan.

If readers like Mrs Carola Smith of North Kessock were saddened by what she described as rather petty comments in the Courier's leader column – which, to Miss Barron's credit, she printed albeit with a characteristically waspish Editor's Note – they must have been impressed by the amount of column inches dedicated to the theatre opening and gala.

The pipes and drums of the Gordon Highlanders, then stationed at nearby Fort George, played outside as ticket-holders arrived and scores of hopefuls queued in the hope of returns or standing places at the historic event.

The regiment's trumpeters provided the opening fanfare as Andrew Cruickshank cut the ceremonial ribbon. Recalling his first exposure to drama and music as a student in Aberdeen where he had seen Matheson Lang at His Majesty's and John Barbirolli conducting in the Music Hall, the guest of honour congratulated those who had created Eden Court for their foresight and courage and hoped it would provide a similar introduction to music and drama for generations of Highlanders.

The hesitant raising of the safety curtain caused the designers some anxious moments. "This had only been fitted during the previous week and, when raised for the first time, had jammed against the masonry of the fly-tower which had to be cut away to allow it free passage," Sir James Dunbar-Nasmith recalled. "Obviously this created a lot of

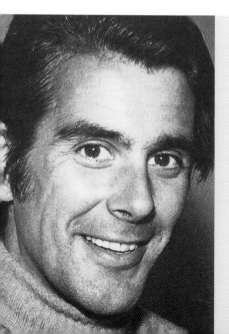

Above
Opening Gala programme and covers from the early days.

Left
Inverness-born Donald MacLeary, a principal dancer with the Royal Ballet, and later coach to prima ballerina Darsey Bussell, was invited to appear at the opening gala.

Right
The author's invitation to the Gala Opening.

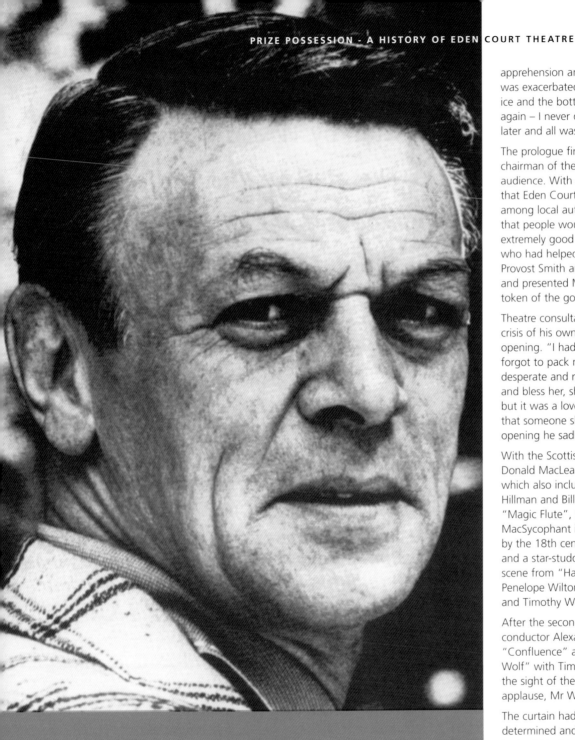

Above
The first actor to speak on the Eden Court stage, Russell Hunter brought several one-man shows to the theatre and returned in "Krapp's Last Tape" almost 25 years to the day of the theatre's anniversary.

apprehension among those who knew of the problem, which was exacerbated when it rose sufficiently to expose the dry ice and the bottom half of Russell Hunter, then dropped again – I never discovered why. It rose properly a few seconds later and all was well for the rest of the evening."

The prologue finally delivered, Provost Fraser – by then chairman of the theatre's board of governors – welcomed the audience. With characteristic understatement, he observed that Eden Court had caused "considerable discussion" among local authorities and the public but he was confident that people would come to recognise they had received extremely good value for £1.9m. He paid tribute to all those who had helped bring the theatre into being, notably the late Provost Smith and the late Bailie Baxter for their foresight, and presented Mr Cruickshank with a souvenir quaich as a token of the governors' appreciation.

Theatre consultant John Wyckham was faced with a minor crisis of his own when he arrived in Inverness for the gala opening. "I had the shirt, tie and trousers but my late wife forgot to pack my dinner jacket," he recalled. " I was desperate and rang Margaret Baxter to see if she could help, and bless her, she offered me Dougie's jacket. It was a bit big but it was a lovely gesture – and I thought how appropriate that someone should have been wearing his jacket at the opening he sadly never lived to see!"

With the Scottish National Orchestra in the orchestra pit, Donald MacLeary and Doreen Wells opened the programme which also included Scottish Opera singers Patricia Hay, David Hillman and Bill McCue performing arias from Mozart's "Magic Flute", Russell Hunter returning as Sir Pertinax MacSycophant in an excerpt from "The Man Of The World" by the 18th century Scots actor-manager Charles Macklin, and a star-studded Prospect Theatre Company performing a scene from "Hamlet" with Derek Jacobi in the title role, Penelope Wilton as Ophelia, Moira Redmond as Gertrude and Timothy West as Claudius.

After the second interval, the Scottish National Orchestra and conductor Alexander Gibson took the stage to premiere "Confluence" and to perform Prokofiev's "Peter And The Wolf" with Timothy West as narrator. Much to his delight, the sight of the extended stage was greeted with a round of applause, Mr Wyckham recalled.

The curtain had risen on Eden Court but with the cost now determined and the arrangements for payment resolved, it had yet to allay fears about the running costs it would incur.

Act Two of Eden Court's history was about to begin and the critics' pens were still poised.

"WHAT EDEN COURT COURT MEANS TO ME"

CLIO GOULD *SCOTTISH ENSEMBLE*

"...We always enjoy playing at Eden Court. The theatre acoustic is very lively and the audience is very welcoming and enthusiastic."

"We always enjoy playing at Eden Court. The theatre acoustic is very lively and the audience is very welcoming and enthusiastic. We have seen numbers increase steadily over the years. We've had out fair share of eventful performances at Eden Court but the most memorable has to be in February 2000 when we performed our American programme "Applachian Spring" which, apart from the famous Copland piece, included Barber's very popular "Adagio For Strings". We played to nearly 700 people – a great increase from our first audience of 90 only 18 months earlier."

Below
Actor Timothy West played Claudius and narrated "Peter and the Wolf" at Eden Court's Opening Gala.

CHAPTER SEVEN

ANOTHER OPENING, ANOTHER SHOW

In 1976, the 400th anniversary of the opening of England's first public playhouse, Burbage's Theatre in London, five new theatres opened in Britain – the National Theatre's Olivier, Lyttelton and Cottesloe theatres in London, the Royal Exchange, Manchester, and Eden Court.

The new Scottish theatre attracted considerable press attention, not only North and South of the Border. The opening was also reported in the South China Post!

"If the shows presented within these walls are as good as the facilities that have been provided, then Eden Court might even upstage the Loch Ness Monster," the Scotsman's distinguished arts editor, Allen Wright commented. After attending the performance of "The Importance of being Earnest", he added: "To visit this building on the banks of the Ness would be a pleasure, even if it provided entertainment of indifferent quality. On this occasion, we are twice blessed…"

"Inverness has now on its hands one of the most sophisticated theatres in the country – the inside is spellbinding, truly thrilling," the Sunday Times declared. "A triumphant fact – a pleasure dome, perhaps, on the riverside," The Guardian stated.

Eden Court was certainly making a favourable impression. Even a local Free Church minister spoke on "the good reputation which Eden Court has built up" – but he deplored its decision to stage "Hair" which had gained some notoriety because some performers appeared naked in the final tableau, describing it as, "a pornographic show".

In a letter to the editor of the Courier, Mr Alistair Hamilton, Oxford, wrote: "The important decisions are now history and Inverness has a multi-purpose building which is superbly equipped to fill its many potential roles. It is also the only modern building in Inverness to show any evidence of care in its external design.

"So far as the community is concerned, the most important thing is that it should be used and succeed as a cultural centre for the area. Invernessians and the wider Highland community now have the opportunity to use the theatre to broaden their horizons and awareness and to escape the introversion and elitism which so often characterises the town and for which you (the Editor) appear determined to remain as guardian."

Jake Bell of Hammersmith, London, congratulated the people of Inverness on possessing a facility like Eden Court. "The whole project seems to exemplify the Scots capacity for matching liveliness of imagination with a serious sense of practicalities and shows a generous thoroughness in the actual building," he went on. "I spend much of my working time visiting community, university and civic arts centres but have yet to be as impressed as by my visit to Eden Court."

Even if a broken lock delayed Grampian TV presenter Kennedy Thomson's official launch of the SCDA Festival, adjudicator Adrian Rendle had high praise for the building and many of the programmes – like the SNO concert, "A Girl In My Soup" and the Royal Lyceum's Scots comedy, "The Flou'rs O' Edinburgh" which starred Roddy MacMillan and John Grieve, repeating their successful double act from TV's "Para Handy", and was directed by Bill Bryden, then at the start of an illustrious stage career, which was to take him to London's National Theatre – were attracting large audiences and favourable reviews in the local press.

Even with Eden Court in full swing, other events continued to be held elsewhere. America's Sara Grey appeared at the Folk Club, Max Houliston at the Fiddle & Accordion Club,

Left
Jimmy Logan makes up as Dame for Eden Court's pantomime "Dick Whittington" in December 1976.

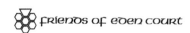

FRIENDS OF EDEN COURT

First Anniversary

EDEN COURT THEATRE

DINNER
AND
DANCE
WITH
CABARET

BY

**Alastair
McDonald**

15th APRIL 1977

Left and above
Programme covers for the years of 1976, '77 and '78 and later.

Inverness Jazz Platform was launched by Ken Hyder's trail-blazing Celtic-jazz fusion band, Talisker, and the Hillsiders returned to the Country & Western Club.

But within a month of the theatre's opening, warning bells were beginning to ring behind the scenes. On Monday 17th May, Inverness District Council's Policy & Resources Committee were buoyed by the news that the Scottish Office had approved borrowing consent of £520,000 for the balance of the theatre's capital costs but was disturbed to hear that running costs were running away. The theatre director had already spent most of his budget for certain services with nine months of the financial year still to run.

Conscious of public sensitivity over Eden Court finances, members called for tighter controls but Councillor Ron Lyon said Mr Edwards should be treated the same as other directors of council departments whose spending was not monitored on a regular basis. Chief executive Ian Miller agreed running a theatre was not like running other Council departments. Flexibility was required but tighter control was necessary, he said. The full Council considered the matter on 24th May and agreed its finance director should keep an eye on the situation.

The Council also learned that the Scottish Arts Council was to contribute £35,000 to the theatre's running costs in the first year and that the autumn programme would include the Northern Meeting piping competitions, a Country & Western Club concert, Jimmy Logan's one-man show, "Lauder", the Jim MacLeod Band, The Corries, Ballet Rambert, the return of the Scottish Chamber Orchestra and a Christmas concert by members of Northern Constabulary. Eden Court was also to stage its first Christmas pantomime, "Dick Whittington", starring Jimmy Logan and pop star Paul Jones.

"That was the first time I'd ever appeared with a male principal boy," Jimmy Logan recalled. "He was the one that really convinced me it could work because he was so believable. Everyone was worried about the reaction of children who'd never seen a big pantomime in a theatre before. How would they know how to respond? – but panto is basically good against evil and the kids instinctively want the goodies to win.

"There's a technique to panto that gets the children involved without letting them take control – although they did get out of hand one year and start throwing sweeties at the stage. I had

to go out at the interval and give them a lecture…
'Stop, or else!'"

The veteran Scottish comic and actor proved so popular with the Highland public, he returned for three more pantomimes. "One Christmas, the computer at the Town Hall broke down and there was no money to pay the cast," he revealed. "I had to threaten the theatre manager who took the night's takings from the box office to pay the artsists and staff something."

On 28th May 1976, Eden Court's Management Committee discovered that the theatre's box office returns in the first six weeks of operation had not matched expectations and showed a deficit of £3017 compared to estimates. Edwards assured them the theatre wasn't "rushing to doom" and was confident the budget would be met.

On 1st June, under the headline "Former Council Criticised", the Courier reported that Russell Johnston had received a response from Mr McElhone about his concern that misleading statements may have been given to the public about Eden Court's capital costs.

The Scottish Under-Secretary agreed that evidence led on behalf of the Council at the public inquiry in September 1974 suggested that the Council had a fixed price contract for Eden Court. "Technically this should have been described as a 'firm price' contract and this was the type of contract received by the Department at the time," he stated.

The Minister accepted that the dramatic increase in costs was attributed to delays and renegotiations arising from the bankruptcy of the original steel sub-contractor and the delay in finding a successor at a time of a three-day week and severe shortage of steel.

"Under the conditions of the contract, which were the standard conditions on all such contracts, the main contractor was able to submit a successful claim for an extension of the time for the completion of the contract and for reimbursement of losses and expenses occurred," he added.

"It is not clear why the representatives for the former Inverness Town Council did not mention at the Inquiry the possibility of such claims being made by the main contractor since the bankruptcy and other events had occurred some months earlier. The Secretary Of State's knowledge of the situation at that time, however, largely depended upon the report he received from the Reporter at the Inquiry and upon the evidence given at the Inquiry.

The Green Lady

Over the years, many theatregoers could justifiably claim Eden Court as a regular haunt – but only The Green Lady genuinely haunts the place.

Val Falcon, Theatre Manager, is convinced she saw the ghost soon after the theatre opened. "The show had just gone in and I was talking to two of the usherettes in the stalls foyer when I saw a woman in what I took to be a green trouser suit coming up the stairs. I asked one of the usherettes to look after the late-comer but when she went round the corner there was no one there.

"On another occasion, the show had finished and everyone had left. I was in the bar with a couple of the staff when we heard footsteps on what we call 'The Street' – the ground-floor foyer. I thought somebody had got locked in and went to let them out but when I got into the foyer, once again, there was no-one there.

"On two occasions, when we've hung an exhibition in the foyer gallery, we've gone back to find a picture has fallen on the floor – yet the hooks that were holding them to the display rods were intact and in place.

"David Carruthers had an Afghan Hound which he took to work every day. It followed him everywhere – but it would never go into the hall of the Bishop's Palace," Val added. "If David was going that way, Shane would screech to a halt at the door and his hairs would bristle.

"Other people have had similar experiences and if I'm moving around the theatre on my own and feel an atmosphere, I'll say 'It's all right, it's only me' and carry on. I don't know if it reassures the Green Lady – but it certainly reassures me."

After her initial experiences Val talked to other people, including nurses who had lived in The Bishop's Palace, and they agreed it was haunted, reputedly by the wife of the bishop and that the garden had been haunted by the ghost of a child with a candle.

No one, however, has seen a child with a candle in what is now the car park – but Eden Court's elusive Green Lady maintains an honourable tradition of the British stage where the expression "The ghost walks" signified pay-day.

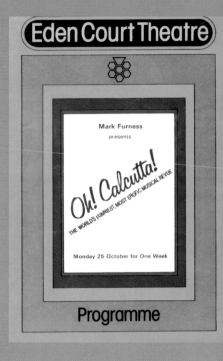

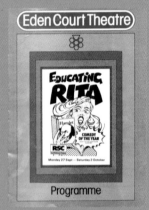

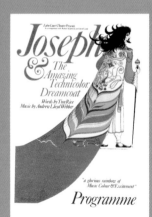

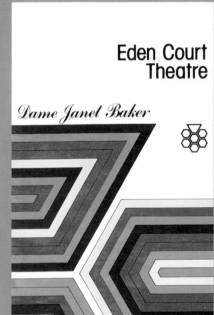

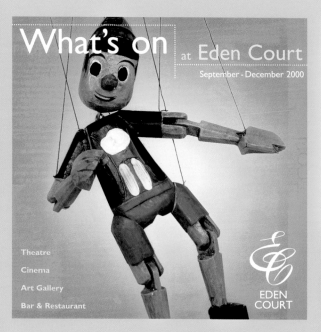

eft to right
den Court programme covers
rom 1977 to 1997

Above
Eden Court programme covers
from 1997 onwards.

Above
Ex-Manfred Mann vocalist Paul Jones proved a male principal boy could 'work' in Eden Court's first pantomime "Dick Whittington". He has revisited the theatre many times, including March 2001, with the Blues Band.

"As regards the future, the statutory provisions under which the Inquiry was held and the necessity to obtain borrowing consent were repealed and in their place Section 94 of the 1973 Local Government (Scotland) Act provides that it should not be lawful for a local authority to incur any liability to meet capital expenditures without the consent of the Secretary Of State".

"This section will mean that in future, a local authority would require to obtain the Secretary Of State's consent before entering into any similar contract to that of the contract for Eden Court Theatre, but the Secretary Of State does not require to hold a Public Inquiry before granting such consent. A situation directly comparable to the Eden Court Inquiry is therefore unlikely to arise again."

"Eden Court now exists and I for one am very happy that it does," Mr Johnston commented. "I also think that by following this matter through, one should make sure that no similar misunderstanding will arise anywhere else in the future."

Twenty-five years later, the "fixed-price contract" riddle still intrigues conspiracy theorists. When asked, ex-Provost William Fraser looked blank and said he could not explain how the impression was created. Nor could Derek Bigg.

The minutes of the special Council meeting which approved the contract on 26th March 1973 make no mention of a fixed price contract, although the preceding reference to the theatre project in the minutes of the Provost's Committee of 10th January is a masterpiece in the art of bureaucratic inscrutability: "The Town Clerk reported on certain developments which had taken place with reference to the building contract for Eden Court and was instructed by the committee as to the appropriate action to be taken".

The first public reference to the alleged deal seems to have been made by the late Provost Smith. The term was subsequently used by the Council's QC at the public inquiry and adopted by the Reporter in his findings in fact. Even the District's Chief Executive used the expression in a letter to the region's joint director of law and administration, Ronald Stevenson, on 24th September 1975 when he informed him of the "increase in Cruden Ltd's fixed price contract notified to the District Council on 23rd July".

The controversial firm/fixed price contract may remain a source of some embarrassment but, twenty-six years on, Ex-Provosts William Fraser and Allan Sellar maintained there had been no attempt to mislead council colleagues or the public. Accountant Hamish Bauchop, who joined the Town Council in 1973 and became the keenest scrutineer of Eden Court's accounts and most outspoken critic of its financial control, agreed. "There was nothing sinister about it," he declared. "It was a misunderstanding."

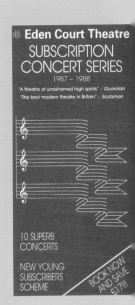

Left to right
More covers from the past (left) and present (right) for the Concert Series

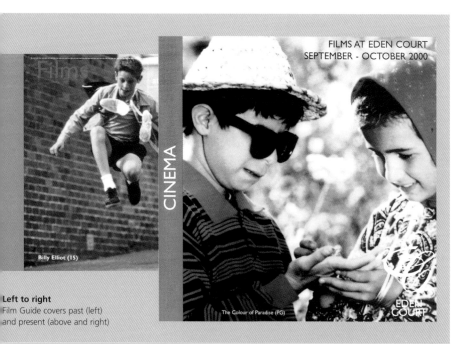

FILMS AT EDEN COURT
SEPTEMBER - OCTOBER 2000

CINEMA

Billy Elliot (15)

The Colour of Paradise (PG)

EDEN COURT

Left to right
Film Guide covers past (left)
and present (above and right)

Russian Fantasy

Eden
Court
Theatre

INTERNATIONAL
MUSIC
SERIES
'88/'89

25TH ANNIVERSARY

Concert
SERIES

EDEN COURT CONCERT SUBSCRIPTION SERIES
SEPTEMBER 2001 - MAY 2002

25
ANNIVERSARY

EDEN
COURT

"WHAT EDEN COURT COURT MEANS TO ME"

SIR CAMERON MACKINTOSH

"I'm delighted the theatre is doing well under its new management and reaching out into the community.'

"I was very pleased to bring "Five Guys Named Moe" to Eden Court five years ago. The management at that time left something to be desired – but the show worked very well and the audience had a great time. I'm delighted the theatre is doing well under its new management and reaching out into the community. What they are doing sounds exactly right and, as one of the theatre's new Patrons, I'll do what I can to help. I'd like to bring more shows to Eden Court but I've nothing on the scale of "Five Guys Named Moe". Something like "Cats" would be perfect – but unfortunately the auditorium and the catchment area are not big enough to cover the costs.

CHAPTER EIGHT

CRISIS MANAGEMENT

In Leatherhead, Murray Edwards had administered the production of the Thorndyke Theatre's own shows and, 25 year later, he admitted that he had no experience of programming a receiving house like Eden Court.

"I had a preliminary interview with John Wyckham in Epsom who must have talked to all the applicants and drew up a short list for the Council to interview," Edwards recalled. "That was before the full Council in the Council Chamber and I remember one of the questions they asked me was 'Would you present the musical "Hair" at Eden Court?' and I gave the political answer which was "If I though the time was right, yes I would".

"Some time later, I was on my way to the station to catch the London sleeper when Alistair Milne came riding along on his bicycle, spotted me, screeched to a halt and said: 'You got the job!' So I knew I had been successful before I left Inverness."

One of the first things the young director had to do when he moved into his tiny temporary office in the Town House was to draw up a budget for the theatre's running costs. "Everybody had been so concerned about the capital cost of the building, they hadn't given a thought to the running costs," he said.

"I had to calculate how much it was all likely to cost and put an application into the Scottish Arts Council which I don't think had put any price on its future involvement in Eden Court but it recognised its responsibility to one of the first new theatres in Scotland and came up with a contributory grant in return for SAC nominees on the Board of Governors – of whom Peter Donald was the first – and, as has happened in other places I've been, it didn't go down well when the Council realised they would have to subsidise the running costs too.

"My second job was to attempt to put a programme together with the Governors saying this is what Inverness wants and the Arts Council telling me what it expected too.

"I would have to be honest and say this was something I hadn't done in my life before but I was Scottish and knew people on the Scottish theatre scene. I was also fortunate in that the Scottish National Orchestra, Scottish Opera and Scottish Ballet who, when canvassed for their opinions, had all said it was essential for Inverness to have a theatre and when it finally got one they were obliged to deliver product for it."

As he told the inaugural meeting of the theatre Governors on 26th October 1976 when asked why box office returns were falling short of the estimates, Edwards admitted he was working in the dark. There was little or no basis for comparison when estimating the size of an audience likely to be attracted to certain shows. The theatre was also short of staff, which increased to the deficit between the income and expenditure columns in the theatre's revenue budget.

The following month, faced with the potential deficit of £50,000, the board appointed a sub-committee to monitor the situation. Councillor Hamish Bauchop wondered where the money would come from but Councillor Roland Mardon said it was still early days and the Governors shouldn't panic. Crawfords, a national catering company operating the restaurant, also reported it was making a loss.

In her leader, Miss Barron could not forbear from saying "I told you so". "For good or ill, the place is there and it is too early to say that it would save more money to close it down than it would make kept open," she added in her leader of 19th November.

Left
In 1990, Glasnost and Perestroika brought Moscow City Ballet to Eden Court where it rehearsed and premiered its production of "Don Quixote" prior to undertaking a UK tour and staging it back home.

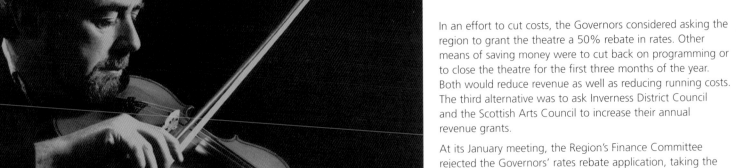

In an effort to cut costs, the Governors considered asking the region to grant the theatre a 50% rebate in rates. Other means of saving money were to cut back on programming or to close the theatre for the first three months of the year. Both would reduce revenue as well as reducing running costs. The third alternative was to ask Inverness District Council and the Scottish Arts Council to increase their annual revenue grants.

At its January meeting, the Region's Finance Committee rejected the Governors' rates rebate application, taking the view that ratepayers were already contributing enough to the theatre through paying loan charges – but it recognised that if the Governors succeeded in their plan to obtain charitable status for the theatre, the Region would be obliged to grant the rate rebate.

The bid to obtain charitable status was opposed at meetings of the theatre's board and the District Council by Councillor Bauchop who said it could have a detrimental effect on the operation of the theatre's restaurant and bars and on programming, which would have to be of an educational nature.

In February, the Governors accepted the theatre director's recommendation that seat prices by increased by 20% in line with inflation. Councillor Skinner wryly observed some people would be prepared to pay a lot more to see the likes of French heart-throb Sacha Distel.

Eden Court's audiences, meanwhile, were still acquainting themselves with new pleasures. On 2nd March 1977, for the second of three appearances in three months, the Scottish Baroque Ensemble performed Vivaldi's "Four Seasons" and the audience, unaware that it was a series of four three-movement concertos, dutifully applauded after four movements, unaware that "Summer" had just begun. The ensemble's leader, the late Leonard Friedman, looked even more bemused than usual – but not as bemused as he must have felt when the Courier referred to him in a subsequent review as "Leonard Bernstein"!

That month, the theatre's financial plight was reduced when Inverness District Council decided to increase its annual grant to £137,250, the Scottish Arts Council increased its funding to £48,000 and the Governors found savings of almost £10,000. Despite strong objections from Councillor Bauchop, the board decided to proceed with an application for charitable status and to increase the cost of hiring the theatre, despite protests from local amateur companies.

Andrew Cruickshank returned to the theatre as part of a star-studded bill for Eden Court's first Royal Gala attended by Princess Alexandra. Also on the bill were Aly Bain, Jimmy Logan's jazz-singing sister Annie Ross, Barbara Dickson and Vince Hill. The performance raised £5000 for the Provost's Benevolent Fund.

Despite the approval of its Policy & Resources Committee, the District decided to take legal advice on the consequences of charitable status and, on 30th May, the Region deferred its decision – despite objections from Councillor Aileen Dekker, a theatre's governor who promoted chamber music concerts at her Auldearn home. She said programming at Pitlochry Theatre was unaffected by its charitable status.

In their quarterly Newsletter, Friends Of Eden Court expressed concern that they couldn't register as a charity unless the theatre could – and they couldn't therefore obtain tax relief on the money they raised for Eden Court.

Billy Connolly made his Eden Court debut on 21st June and found fresh material in firebrand Glasgow preacher Pastor Jack Glass who picketed the theatre, claiming that Connolly was a blasphemer. Needless to say, the fundamentalist clergyman found his way into the act – but the Courier found the comedian's jokes "distasteful and of a very low standard" and, in its next issue, had to apologise to Pastor Glass for a misprint in its coverage of his protest. "He did not carry an orange banner but an ornate banner", it stated.

Expensive though it was, 25 years on, Murray Edwards still believed his policy of bringing famous names to Eden Court was the right one. "It was a question of establishing the theatre not only in the minds of the Highland public but impressing performers and their agents that there was now another theatre on the Scottish circuit and I think we were successful in doing that," he declared.

"I was incredibly lucky to get Jimmy Logan for the first pantomime. He happened to be free that year and it needed someone of his calibre to establish pantomime at Eden Court. Some of the internationally famous classical artists I booked, people like James Galway and Sviatoslav Richter, would have come in through the SNO or SCO because they would have been touring with them anyway – but in the time I was there we also had people like Victor Borge, Stephan Grappelli, Paco Pena, Los Paraguayos, Marian Montgomery & Richard Rodney Bennett, Marty Robbins, Carl Perkins and Bo Diddley, The Boys Of The Lough, Alasdair Gilies, The Corries, Ronnie Corbett, The Bachelors, The New Seekers, Hinge & Bracket, the Syd Lawrence Orchestra, Ballet Rambert, D'Oyly Carte

Above left
Scots fiddler Aly Bain opened Eden Court's first star-studded charity gala before an audience that included Princess Alexandra.

Bottom left
Billy Connolly found a ready source of material when fundamentalist preacher Pastor Jack Glass picketed his Eden Court show.

Right
With folksinger Alistair MacDonald and fiddler Alasdair Fraser, legendary Scots comedian Chic Murray was one of the stars of Eden Court's first Summer Season.

and shows like "The Importance Of being Earnest", "A Midsummer Night's Dream" and "Godspell".

"Not everything did well, of course – the Oxford Playhouse production of "The Country Wife" didn't attract a big audience although it was a good show – but, with no track record and a lot of interest, we had to encourage people to come long distances and the shows we put in did have people flying in from the Islands and driving down from Thurso."

Eden Court was not restricted to professional use, however. Inverness Opera Company was the first amateur company to use the theatre with its March 1977 production of "The Mikado" and Edwards encouraged local musicians and singers to use informal lunchtime events in the stalls foyer as a showcase.

Among the first groups to use the theatre were the local traditional jazz band, The Ness River Rhythm Kings, formed a year earlier, Inverness Opera Company which staged songs from the shows – the young Janis Kelly's compelling performance of "Send In The Clowns" clearly revealed her potential when she graduated from the Royal Scottish Academy of Music & Drama – and Inverness Jazz Platform who promoted local jazz groups in various styles.

The first amateur drama company to perform on the stage was The Florians. "We did Agatha Christie's 'Ten Little Indians'," Jimmy Pringle recalled. "We played to 800 people in three nights – the biggest audience we'd ever had. We couldn't believe it. Because it was in Eden Court, people must have thought they were going to see a professional company."

The Alexander Brothers and Jack Milroy starred in Eden Court's second Summer Season.

Despite the setbacks over seeking charitable status, the Governors re-affirmed their view that it was essential, despite continued opposition from Councillor Bauchop. At the board meeting of 1st July 1977, he said the Governors should continue to seek a discretionary rate rebate from the Regional Council but Councillor Drummond pointed out that under charitable status, the rebate would be recoverable from the government through the Council's annual Rates Support Grant and would not be borne by the ratepayer.

Tony Wraight, the SAC's drama director and first assessor on the board, said many Scottish theatres had charitable status and that the Arts Council strongly supported the Governors' decision to apply. In a letter to the Courier, Derek Bigg, by then chief internal auditor at the Highland Health Board, pointed out that charitable status would reduce the rates by 1p in the pound. Later that month, both District and Region Councils acceded to the Governors' request.

On 29th August, ex-Provost MacKay died but tributes listing his accomplishments overlooked the part he had played in the genesis of Eden Court Theatre.

Meanwhile there was a capacity audience for Richter, an eccentric genius regarded by many as the finest pianist of the time. On September 12th, 1977, he appeared at Eden Court to play Beethoven, Chopin and Debussy on his preferred Yamaha piano which accompanied everywhere on tour – even as far north as Inverness. That autumn brought D'Oyly Carte back to Inverness for the first time since 1898 when the company made the last of its regular visits to the Theatre Royal. Slim Whitman, Rod McKuen and the BBC Scottish Symphony Orchestra conducted by a skinny, tousle-headed 22-year-old called Simon Rattle were among the theatre's other autumn attractions.

Far left
Another Scots-born funnyman, Ronnie Corbett was one of the first national TV personalities to appear at Eden Court.

Left
With comedian Jack Milroy, The Alexander Brothers starred in Eden Court's second Summer Season.

Above
Hailed as the greatest pianist of the century, Russian virtuoso Sviatoslav Richter brought his own piano to Eden Court when he appeared in recital.

Above
 Scotland's master of music, Sir Alexander Gibson, conducted the Scottish
National Orchestra in a powerful performance of Nielsen's Fourth
Symphony, "The Inextinguishable", and left an inextinguishable memory.

A fey American singer-songwriter, McKuen attracted
headlines in a Sunday newspaper by blaming high prices for
a half-empty auditorium. Edwards retorted that tickets would
not have been so much if McKuen's fee had been less.

On 26th October, the Governors learned that the Inland
Revenue had granted the theatre charitable status and the
following month a visual arts element was added to Eden
Court when a sculpture by Gavin Scobie representing Ben
Nevis and commissioned by the Scottish Arts Council was
installed outside the building. Painting and photographic
exhibitions in the theatre foyer have always been a feature of
Eden Court.

Despite its reservations about the cost of Eden Court,
the Courier reviewed every performance. Miss Barron herself
covered classical music, opera and ballet. Senior reporter
Lachlan Ross reviewed drama and died two days before
he was able to give his verdict on Eden Court's
second pantomime.

Scottish Ballet's production of "The Nutcracker" followed in
January and, during the visit, the Highlands was hit by its
worst blizzard in 25 years. Scottish Ballet had to cancel
performances and, with the A9 blocked, it was several days
before the company's traction units were able to return to
Inverness for the company's sets. On the final day of the
performance, One of Eden Court's stage doormen, Nick
Quinn – a popular figure with theatre staff and performers –
finished his shift and set off to drive home to Farr. His car
became stuck in the snow and he tried to complete his
journey on foot but, overcome by exhaustion, he collapsed
and died in the snow.

"That was the saddest thing," Val Falcon, the theatre's
former chief usherette and present manager, recalled. "I
asked him to stay the night with my husband and me but he
wanted to get home. My last words to him were: 'If the
road's too bad, come back'."

Later that month, the Governors heard that savings and
increased box office income had reduced the theatre's deficit
from £34,730 and £27,230. "Scotland The What" proved a
popular attraction but despite full houses the costlier Dave
Allen and Dutch Swing College Jazz Band failed to reduce
the deficit and on 15th February, the Governors appeal for
£150,000 – a 10% increase in the District Council's grant –
was rejected. Hamish Bauchop said the theatre's patrons
should pay more for their pleasures.

"It is misleading to talk about subsidies," the future Provost
and chairman of the Governors, Councillor Allan Sellar, said.

'If Eden Court was a commercial theatre, there would be no need for a subsidy – but there would be no opera or ballet either."

Crawfords gave up the restaurant franchise and it was taken over by David and Kristine Mackenzie who acquired a reputation with their Struy restaurant "Kristine's Kitchen" – but they immediately caused an uproar among Eden Court patrons with their prices.

Moves were now afoot for Eden Court to absorb the TIE-Up Theatre Company, which would become the theatre's touring and educational unit. Councillor Skinner welcomed the proposal, which would bring drama to schoolchildren and people in outlying areas. In March, Murray Edwards announced that the theatre had received a Scottish Arts Council grant for this purpose and additional funds were being sought from the Highland Board and other sources. "The Wizard Of Oz", "The Importance Of Being Earnest", "MacBeth" and "Joseph And His Amazing Technicolor Dreamcoat" were to be among the productions.

Edwards recognised that touring was an essential way to promote Eden Court in other parts of the Highlands and elsewhere in Scotland. The theatre's production of "Joseph" played to capacity houses in Stirling, Aberdeen and Edinburgh, earning valuable revenue and publicity for the Inverness theatre and other shows produced by John Doyle toured closer to home.

The main stage played host to the Scottish National Orchestra, whose performance under Sir Alexander Gibson of Nielsen's Fourth Symphony, "The Inextinguishable", remains one of the most memorable events ever held at Eden Court. A touring production of "Hair" had a week's run – Edwards obviously considered the time was right – but the notorious nude scene was very brief and there were few shocks, the Courier noted.

Inverness singer Louise Kelly – later to return in pantomime – joined Peter Morrison and Johnnie Beattie for Eden Court's third summer show. Laryngitis prevented the Duchess Of Kent from attending a charity royal gala given by the Scottish Chamber Orchestra, the Highland Strathspey & Reel Society staged a 75th anniversary concert and Rikki Fulton had been signed for the forthcoming "Cinderella" when, in October 1979, Edwards announced that he was leaving to take up an appointment with Sir Bernard Miles's celebrated Mermaid Theatre in London.

Before he left, however, it was revealed that the theatre's deficit was now running at £31,266 and Governors were

Right
Val Falcon, the head usherette who became Theatre Manager of the theatre, holds the unique distinction of having twenty-five years service at the 25 year old theatre.

Left
Wrestling with underfunding – Provost Allan Sellar who inherited the hot seat as chairman of Inverness District Council and Eden Court's Board Of Governors.

Left
Inverness singer Louise Kelly co-starred in the third Summer Season and returned as 'Maid Marian' in pantomime.

Left
Simon Rattle served his apprenticeship with the BBC Scottish Symphony Orchestra and the Scottish Chamber Orchestra, appearing with each at Eden Court.

"There was a will for the place to succeed and I'm sure if it had been a small, no-name, middle of the road place, it wouldn't have done. As I said when I left, the intention was to get if off at the right level and that is the legacy of the early years. It gave all of us a lot of heartache at the time but when you kick off a new organisation, you have to kick off at a level it needs to survive – and it has. And this wasn't Leeds or Birmingham, it was Inverness – 110 miles from the nearest population centre!"

His view was endorsed by theatre consultant John Wyckham, "No matter how good the theatre building, so much of the success or failure of keeping it going depends on the first six months," he declared. "I've seen it happen elsewhere, if you don't book a range of first class attractions, it will die – and much of the credit for establishing Eden Court with artists and audiences must go to the first director."

By December 1978 the deficit had accumulated to £50,000 and to ensure the theatre's continuing operation, Inverness District Council agreed to an advance on the following year's grant. Members were told the situation did not arise from overspending and the Governors were trying to obtain a substantial increase in grant from the Arts Council.

"Cinderella" attracted capacity audiences but did not show a profit – with two dames and the spectacular transformation scene, this most popular panto is regarded as the most expensive to produce – and by January the Eden Court's deficit had grown to £70,000. The Governors responded by cutting overheads by £30,000, scaling down the next panto and cutting back on Eden Court Theatre Company productions. Visits by Pitlochry Festival Theatre Company and two SCO concerts were dropped.

Some of Edwards' choices proved to be utter disasters. "'The Song Of The Hump-Back Whale" attracted an audience of three – "and two of them were Press," Val Falcon recalled "As a result, we had to switch that performance from the auditorium to the foyer – which is what we had to do for a concert of electronic music. The sounds were so strange, one woman in the audience started shaking with silent laughter and that set everyone else off!"

Despite the losses, Edwards' achievements were recognised with a parting gift and his farewell gala, which reflected the story of Eden Court so far, was sold out. Michael Jones, an arts and entertainments officer from Hertfordshire, was appointed to succeed him but he may have got cold feet when he learned of the theatre's financial plight and backed out.

concerned and angry when their treasurer, Alan Imlah, said it was unlikely to be reduced. "We can't afford losses on this scale; we must do something," Councillor Bauchop declared. Blame was placed on the poor box office returns for Scottish Opera and the Pitlochry Festival Theatre season. Edwards said he had already asked for more well-known operas and warned against spending cuts that would diminish the quality of the panto.

"It's easy to be wise after the event and, in hindsight, it may not have been the right thing to do," Edwards commented 22 years later. "In the cold grey light of experience, I'd probably have done more things on a shared cost basis – but my youth was against me. I have a lot more contacts now than I had then and I am in a position to call in more favours but I built on the experience of each year and I'm not embarrassed by what happened at that time. I'm convinced Eden Court is what it is now because of the way we established it.

The theatre was facing a deficit of £70,000 when Inverness District Council's Policy and Resources Committee met on February 14 1979 and after the board's secretary, Ronald Stevenson, Highland Regional Council's highly respected Joint Director of Law and Administration, reported that Eden Court's revenue funding needed to be re-appraised, the committee agreed to recommend an extra grant of £50,000 for the current financial year and a 10% increase in the following year's award.

Both were approved at the subsequent meeting of the full Council when the departed Edwards came in for scathing criticism. Labour councillors branded him the "spend, spend, spend" director and accused him of building his reputation at the expense of Inverness ratepayers.

Warning the governors that the Council was not a bottomless pit of finance, they recognised however that a new theatre director and a new spirit among governors presented fresh opportunities to reverse the situation at Eden Court. The optimistic mood was reinforced when the SAC at the Governors' meeting of 22nd March announced an extra £15,000. Director Sandy Dunbar said his council had been impressed by what had been achieved at Eden Court – but warned against a reduction in the artistic content of the theatre's future programme.

Eden Court entered a new financial year in buoyant mood, reinforced by full houses for Humphrey Lyttelton and Stephan Grappelli and the return of Inverness's Royal Ballet star Donald MacLeary who guested with Scottish Ballet on 17th May – but the previous evening Governors received the bombshell news that, despite the extra funds, Eden Court was already £22,000 in the red. A range of options was to be considered at a special meeting in July and the chairman, Provost Ian Fraser, warned of difficult and unpleasant decisions ahead.

The Courier, which had been preoccupied by commenting on the campaign for the Scottish devolution referendum, expressed the hope that the problem of the theatre living beyond its means would be seriously tackled and said the trust set up in memory of Provost Smith – "the prime mover, if not agitator for the theatre" – would be better spending its money on the deficit than on lectures.

The theatre's situation was not improved by the *hiatus* in appointing a successor during which no application was made for the continued funding of John Doyle's production, education and outreach company which folded when the money eventually ran out. Doyle went south to run the Swan

Theatre, Worcester, and Liverpool's Everyman before becoming a freelance director.

Jimmy Logan, who was just finishing his second panto run at Eden Court and had managed his own theatre in Glasgow, offered his advice and assistance to Governors until a permanent appointment could be made – and, on 4th June 1979, Provost Iain Fraser introduced 35 year old Chris Johnson who was to become Eden Court's second director.

He had risen from trainee cinema manager to personal assistant to the managing director of the Rank Organisation before becoming entertainments manger at the Aviemore Centre in 1976 – a career which, the Governors decided, offered them a man with the type of experience now required at Eden Court.

The populist Johnson, who programmed the Centre's cinema/theatre, promoted pop groups in the ballroom and acted as DJ in the discotheque, said he had made money all his business life and while he did not expect the theatre to make a profit, he pledged that it would not run at a loss.

Left
The Board Of Governors benefited when music-lover Ronald Stevenson, The Highland Regional Council's respected chief executive, became Secretary.

Left
Chris Johnson receiving a donation from Friends of Eden Court Treasurer Dorothy Niven, Chairman Dr James Sangster and Organiser Rhona Kirk who as the Friends longest serving Organiser was still in the post in 2001.

Pointing out that his predecessor had programmed the theatre for the next year, Johnson promised something for everybody with a special effort to promote conferences.

"I did know what I was letting myself in for. I had been in Aviemore for three years and I'd read about the constant financial crisis at Eden Court – but, unlike my job at the Aviemore Centre, it presented me with the chance to fully use and develop the management training Rank's had given me and what experience I'd gained in the commercial leisure industry in one of the most marvellous buildings anyone could imagine," Johnson recalled 22 years later.

"It was one of the best opportunities someone in my position could have had 20 years ago and, in spite of some of the question marks over things I did, I really put my best into it. Resources were limited and I had to make the most of what was available on one hand and use a bit of bulls**t and bravado on the other – but, in my view, I ran that building in a way, perhaps the only way, to get it some financial stability and that may not always have been in accordance with the rule book.

"On one or two occasions I started selling tickets for shows before the final contracts were signed. It was the only way I was going to get the big names and the audiences. I trod such a fine line with Max Boyce – but it worked. It got a lot of people into the theatre and proved what it was capable of doing."

Edwards' programming legacy was still being felt, however. The distinguished British actress, Dame Flora Robson appeared on the 6th of June, 1979, which became "D for Darkness Day" when a power cut hit Eden Court during her poetry reading – but the lights didn't go out on Inverness's international jazz singer Jeanie Lamb when she took the stage with the Scottish Jazz Orchestra before a home crowd two nights later.

Two other Inverness performers, Ann Louise Ross and Jimmy Chisholm, lately embarked on professional acting careers, were booked for the next pantomime, "Babes In The Wood", with former Highland SCDA adviser Charles Bell as Dame. Costly star names were not to be involved, the cost-conscious Governors had decided.

There was a full house for Jimmy Logan's comedy "For Love Or Money" – "This is the way it should be," a delighted Chris Johnson declared. "This is why Eden Court is here."

"That's what I liked best – bringing family shows and letting everyone have a good clean laugh," the actor-producer declared in 2001. Over the course of the theatre's first 15 years, no-one was to appear at Eden Court more often than Jimmy Logan, the most enduringly popular entertainer in Scottish show business. He returned with many more of his own productions, often with Scots comedienne Una MacLean as co-star.

Just as the Governors were beginning to think they were finally on top of the financial situation, they learned that the theatre had accumulated a £68,000 deficit and, as a result of the period with no experienced director at the helm, invoices that were not in the accounts were starting to arrive. "Where does it all end?" Councillor Bauchop lamented. Even one of the theatre's most ardent supporters, Robert Fasken, was shaken. "It's an appalling situation," he said.

The Council held a special meeting and agreed to an additional grant of £36,000, which would enable the Governors to buy equipment and foodstocks from the MacKenzies and let the theatre management run the catering service. There was a growing feeling among members that the theatre was not receiving enough support from the Arts Council but Sandy Dunbar said the grant was much the same as Stirling's comparable MacRoberts Centre.

In another bid to cut costs, the Governors decided to rely on imported rather than in-house drama, despite Mr Fasken's concern at the effect on the touring programme but each month the Governors met, they were given the dreaded and headline-grabbing news that the deficit had risen further. Full houses from Chris Barber, Max Boyce, another royal charity gala headlined by Moira Anderson and Alasdair Gillies, who recorded his next LP "Live at Eden Court" in the theatre, were still outnumbering the horror stories in the press, however.

"We are making too much of this deficit," Councillor Roland Mardon declared and Mr Dunbar urged the Governors to aim to increase the theatre's income. They had pruned expenditure as much as they could, he said.

Stars may not have been given an opportunity to shine on stage but roast chestnuts were on sale outside the theatre and Chris Johnson greeted patrons in a top hat and tails when the traditional Victorian panto opened at the beginning of December 1979. "This is panto!" the Courier said of the show but while it undoubtedly saved money, it did not make as much as expected and the year ended with the Governors asking the Regional Council for a grant towards the repair and maintenance of the building which, Councillor Mackintosh of Mackintosh reminded colleagues, now belonged to the Region. The Council decided to pay the theatre's insurance premiums of £7,000 instead.

Despite an inflationary increase in grant from the District Council and the prospect of an additional £40,000 if the Arts Council would match it, the New Year was to prove the most crisis-ridden in Eden Court's short history. At the end of January, the theatre was £42,000 over budget.

The Governors, ignoring the public who had delivered their verdict with their feet, agreed to have another "no stars" panto the next year, much to the alarm of Chris Johnson. He approached Jimmy Logan who agreed to carry out the dual role of star and director in "Aladdin" for a single fee.

"I've been here fairly often and like the area," he told a press conference. "I also appreciate the situation of Eden Court as regards finance. The fact that I'll direct should save some money for Eden Court and Inverness and I see no reason why it shouldn't bring in a penny or two as well."

John Worth was finally to find a role at the theatre as the panto's musical director, writing and arranging music so late into the night that he once fell asleep in the orchestra pit during a performance and had to be gently nudged awake by one of the musicians as the next music cue approached. "That was the old-fashioned way of working and John was a dedicated professional," Jimmy Logan commented. "I tried sending him my music in advance so he would have plenty of time to arrange it, but he still ended up working through the night on it."

Left
Councillor and clan chief Lachlan Mackintosh of Mackintosh, an admirer of George Gershwin, Cole Porter and other great American songwriters, pointed out that Highland Region was obliged to repair and maintain Eden Court – because it owned the building!

The young Inverness actor Jimmy Chisholm was cast as Wishee Washee and proved an ideal foil for the panto veteran's Widow Twanky. "He was very, very good," Logan recalled in 2001. "Last year he was appearing in two plays at Pitlochry when I was doing 'Lauder' and he was superb. As I watched him, I could see the reason why. His pantomime experience was coming through. He knew how to handle an audience and how to time his lines."

The company was struck by tragedy during the final stages of rehearsal when dancer and choreographer Brian Sievwright, a veteran of TV's "White Heather Club", was killed in a road accident on the Inverness-Aberdeen road. "The funeral took place in Aberdeen and the show opened that night," Jimmy Logan recalled. "The performance was dedicated to him and the dancers in the 'Jewel' ballet had tears in their eyes as they performed their tribute to him. It was a very emotional evening."

Johnson, meanwhile, was planning ahead and had booked Jack Jones – but the Board had never heard of the American singer widely regarded as a successor to Sinatra. Nor, it seemed, did his potential audience when he finally appeared some years later. The house was little more than quarter-full – a fact that obviously rankled the star. "Don't keep going on at us," a spectator shouted. "We came!"

Marketing classical concerts containing star names like Menuhin and Galway as a subscription series boosted the box office and levelled attendances at symphony and chamber orchestra concerts – but on 7th March 1980, the Council's General Purposes committee learned the theatre was facing a stark choice.

If the deficit could not be cleared by adequate funding, either the frequency of theatre events would have to be reduced, the theatre would have to be let as a civic hall or it would have to close altogether, vice-chairman Peter Donald warned. Eden Court attracted 145,000 admissions a year and, at the current level of subsidy, cost ratepayers £1 a head, he added. Running it as a hall would increase the per capita cost to an unacceptable level.

James Shaw Grant, a writer and playwright, former member of the HIDB and ex-chairman of the Crofters Commission, said what was needed was a study to determine a realistic level of funding for the theatre. Sensitive about press coverage, Councillor William Fraser declared: "We don't want the media spreading gloom around. We're trying to be constructive."

Top
Inverness-born actor Jimmy Chisholm, a founder member of the cast of the STV soap, "Take The High Road", co-starred with Jimmy Logan in the 1979 pantomime "Aladdin".

Right
Former newspaper editor, playwright and chairman of The Crofters Commission James Shaw Grant was one of the Scottish Arts Council nominees on the theatre's Board Of Governors.

Before the meeting, Provost Ian Fraser had entertained Friends Of Eden Court and thanked them for the £19,000 they had contributed to the theatre over the past three years.

More financial help was forthcoming from local business. Scottish Brewers agreed to sponsor the pantomime to the tune of £6,000 and Marks & Spencer, which had recently opened in the new Eastgate Centre, were to finance a show in the autumn.

The theatre enjoyed another popular success on 21st April when the legendary Yehudi Menuhin appeared with the SNO to play Elgar's violin concerto, which he had recorded as a boy with the composer himself. He offered the delighted crowd a piece of unaccompanied Bach as an encore. The following week, another master violinist, Stephan Grappelli, returned to play to a full house and was charmed when a small girl presented him with a single red rose.

A head-on collision between Council and Governors and the Scottish Arts Council seemed certain on 25th April 1980 when the SAC announced a £10,000 cut in Eden Court's grant and asked the Governors to stop paying subsidised companies a percentage. It should offer them a guarantee instead. Governors protested that they were trying to save money and part of the theatre's problems stemmed from offering guarantees. The SAC should recognise its difficulties and offer a realistic grant, Councillor William Fraser said.

Mr Dunbar offered the theatre an extra £30,000 if the Council would match it and, at the next Board meeting, Governors were told the rate of the deficit increase was finally slowing down.

At the District Council's statutory meeting on 6th May, Councillor Sellar was appointed Provost and chairman of Eden Court's Governors. Donald MacLeary returned to his hometown to guest with Scottish Ballet as Prince Ramiro in "Cinderella" which attracted another full house and helped reduce Eden Court's deficit. George Melly and Harry Secombe were also Eden Court-bound.

On 21st May, the Governors asked the Highland Board to commission an independent study into running and financing the theatre and the following month the Council granted an extra £40,000 which, with the SAC's £30,000, would clear the deficit – but Councillor Bauchop maintained the Arts Council should be meeting the greater proportion of funding for the theatre. Councillor William Fraser noted a welcome improvement in box office returns.

Above
The great Yehudi Menuhin performed his signature piece, Elgar's Violin Concerto, and delighted the audience with an encore of unaccompanied Bach.

Left
In the best interests of the theatre, Arts Council nominee Peter Donald and vice-chairman of the Board took a broad-minded view of Chris Johnson's programming.

Miss Barron was not impressed. "We still consider closure for a short or long period would be a step which could help to rectify the position," she wrote in the Courier. She was impressed, however, by another musical giant, the French cellist Paul Tortelier, who provided a fitting climax to the SCO's 12-day tour of the Highlands with a brilliant performance of Tchaikovsky's Variations On A Rococo Theme and Dvorak's Rondo for Cello. As an encore, he played his own composition "Tears For Sancho".

With the classical element in the 79/80 programme booked by his predecessor, Governors were relying on Johnson's commercial skills but some theatregoers were concerned that his appointment might eventually take Eden Court too far down-market. Their fears were not allayed when snooker stars Steve Davis and Alec "Hurricane" Higgins, all-in wrestlers and a topless revue starring nude model Fiona Richmond appeared in the programme.

"By putting Fiona Richmond on, we did 106% business," Chris Johnson recalled. "People were standing in places the law didn't allow but it brought the money in. They gave the theatre viability and vitality and, to me, made Eden Court a community building. I wanted to make it accessible."

"Peter Donald was very broad-minded about it," ex-Provost Sellar commented. "He knew the theatre had to pay its way and that he couldn't have classical music if he didn't have more popular shows because there wouldn't be a theatre otherwise. Chris was appointed to add a variety that had perhaps been lacking, instead of some of the things some people would regard as fuddy-duddy."

He conceded that the balance did go too far, however, and confirmed that the Scottish Arts Council – notwithstanding the appearances by Dame Janet, Menuhin and Tortelier – expressed concern at the level of arts content of Johnson's programmes. Scott Don, a respected member of Inverness Opera Company and Inverness Choral Society, was more sanguine about the new director, however. "I admired Chris," he said. "He recognised there were some areas where he did not have knowledge – like classical music – and he set up a special committee to advise him on programming.

"The members included Peter Donald, Freddie Lloyd who had recently retired as general manager of the D'Oyly Carte Opera Company and myself – and although we often had different opinions as to what music should be featured, Chris listened to everyone and came up with a programme that was acceptable to everybody."

With the country in the grip of a recession, consequent cuts in local authority spending and the theatre's cumulative deficit topping £100,000 – £44,284 accrued in that financial year – there was little prospect of a much-needed increase in theatre attendances and, in a bid to boost ticket sales, the new theatre director was authorised to offer all seats at the same price at certain performances from the autumn.

In August, Frankie Vaughan drew a full house and opened the Friends Of Eden Court's annual fete. Throwing away the script in favour of uproariously funny ad-libbing, Jimmy Edwards and Eric Sykes played a successful season in "Big Bad Mouse". Despite a £31,000 loss on the summer show, featuring singer/comedian Bill Barclay, Johnson decided to persist with it next year in an attempt to create an institution like its rival, "Summer Showtime", staged annually by John Worth in a local hotel.

Another Johnson initiative, introduced to save staffing costs and reduce the continuing deficit, was to close the theatre on Sundays, transferring the weekly film shows which attracted a small specialised audience from the aditorium to The Long Gallery. The large dressing room on the ground floor of the Bishop's Palace was turned into a makeshift cinema, screening nightly film shows with usherettes doubling in the theatre and the cinema. It was called Second Screen and when funds became available he intended to fully furnish it and use it in summer for a tourist audio-visual show to be called "The Scottish Experience". It was a move that was to have far-reaching implications.

The new director also made a point of being a visible presence in the theatre foyer every evening welcoming patrons on their arrival and listening to their comments on departure. He installed a dance floor in the restaurant and in the stalls foyer and found time to play disc jockey occasionally, revealing an exhibitionist streak by donning a green fright wig and kaftan for the role.

He booked the notoriously full-frontal revue "Oh Calcutta!" – to which the Courier's response was "Oh dear!" – and there was unrest among subscribers to the classical concerts when they couldn't sell or swap unwanted tickets and discovered the series wasn't such a bargain after all. But, despite good business with Boxcar Willie and Val Doonican, the theatre's deficit had soared to £145,000 by November. Johnson also booked a touring production of "Jesus Christ Superstar" and cast TV comic and quiz show host Tom O'Connor, a genial Liverpudlian, as the star of successive pantomimes, including "Cinderella".

A special Governors meeting was held the following month when the Scottish Arts Council said they could hold out little prospect of more cash and Councillor Mardon suggested neighbouring district councils should be asked to help. Miss Barron hit out at Friends "cavorting" at their annual ball while the theatre was in crisis. Chairman, Sheriff Stanley Scott Robinson, Friends' representative on the Board Of Governors, replied that she should support efforts to reverse the theatre's fortunes instead of adopting an unwarranted hypercritical attitude.

In the week Gaelic rock group Runrig made their first sell-out appearance at Eden Court, Inverness District Council decided to give the theatre an £85,000 advance on next year's grant to keep it open over Christmas, despite expectations that the recession would lead to steep rent and rate rises in the New Year.

On 17th December the Governors received the consultants' report, which confirmed that Eden Court was being under funded. Fuller details of the report by Coopers & Lybrand were published early in the New Year and revealed that the theatre had made an operating profit of £52,000 before overheads. Having compared it with five similar theatres in other parts of the country, the consultants found that, despite a smaller catchment population, Eden Court's box office income per seat was £337 compared with £232 elsewhere. Furthermore, no civic theatre in the country was self-supporting.

Although inflation was a factor and there was scope for increasing attendances by altering the balance of the theatre's programming, the report concluded that the level of funding for the theatre was inadequate. Furthermore, operating deficits at the five other theatres were written off or covered by the funding agencies. Managements were replaced if losses were unacceptable.

Coopers & Lybrand also recommended changes in the Governors' role and recommended they meet less often. "In our view the present constitution of the Board is primarily directed to controlling the activities of the theatre rather than promoting them," it noted.

While the report's recommendation were being considered the District Council deliberated changing its policy of renting and not selling sites at the Longman Industrial Estate with the proceeds being used to clear Eden Court's deficit at no cost to ratepayers. Chief Executive Brian Wilson advised that the money should go to the Council's Common Good Fund but, if the Council were so inclined, the theatre's deficit could be wiped out by using the District's accumulated balances.

In February, Governors learned that Moray, Caithness, Sutherland and Gordon district councils had decided against making grants to Eden Court on grounds of distance and, in a letter to the Courier, Inverness accountant Kenneth MacCallum said he hoped the Council would now decide enough was enough and put Eden Court out of its misery.

Right
Full houses for Val Doonican provided a welcome boost at the box office during a troubled time.

"The theatre was based on unrealistic calculations of the potential audience," he declared and pointed out that attendances sometimes failed to reach double figures and that an average of 35% was clearly insufficient to sustain the theatre. "If Eden Court is compelled to close, I will not rejoice since I enjoy all the arts and will regret that, because of initial failures, it will have killed what it ought to have assisted," he concluded.

In her leader of 17th February 1981, Miss Barron suggested Eden Court be turned into a crematorium. "It would, after all, be handy for the subsequent interment of ashes at Tomnahurich Cemetery, scattering them over the river or over the surrounding grass which could easily be transformed into a garden of rest," she declared.

Next day Peter Donald told a special meeting of the Council that Eden Court required at least £240,000 to clear the deficit and could not continue without extra funding – but if the consultants' recommendation were fully implemented, overspending would be eliminated and the theatre would be able to run to budget.

To avert closure, the Council decided on 25th February to award the theatre an annual grant of £244,800 for 1981/82, an increase of £53,000 over the previous year and the equivalent of 0.4p on the rates, and to make a one-off payment of £200,000 from its accumulated balances to meet the deficit, subject to an absolute guarantee that the theatre would run to budget in future.

The motion was put by Councillor William Fraser, later to become Provost and chairman of the board of governors. "I am confident the governors and management can now run the establishment to budget," he told the meeting. "We have also cleared the deficit, so there is now, in my view, no excuse for any further financial problems, barring a major calamity."

"If by April next year the books do not balance, and even more district council aid is required to keep the theatre alive, I will stand down from the Council and the Board."

"In the early years, Eden Court got a lot of money from the Council and I hammered at the management to get it right and sorted once and for all. If they didn't I was certainly going to chuck it," Ex-Provost Fraser declared in 2001. "The council could easily replace me but members recognised I was putting my neck on the block."

Provost Sellar who told the Council he would also resign if the extra half-million for Eden Court proved to no avail. Having taken office only ten months ago, he was undergoing a baptism of fire with Eden Court. "It was a highly charged meeting," he recalled. "Senior councillors said the theatre was incapable of making a profit, we should wash our hands of it, close it down and sell it off. There was all sorts of criticism from both sides of the chamber and, as chairman of the Governors, I just had to sit there and take it – but I knew there was an opportunity to turn Eden Court round.

"When the Coopers & Lybrand report came out, I had poured over the Council accounts with our director of finance, Alan Imlah, and we had found a £200,000 under spend in some account or other. I tipped off Bill Fraser that this money was available and primed him to ensure the under spend should go to Eden Court because I couldn't do it from where I was sitting. He convinced the Council to go along with him."

The strength of their conviction – and their long experience in local government finance – clearly impressed their colleagues. "That was the turning point for Eden Court," declared ex-Provost Sellar. "There's no doubt about it – the theatre would have closed otherwise – but my fellow-governors and I were determined it would it exist and we kept a tight rein on the finances."

Marketing review

119   The Eden Court Theatre is faced, along with the other theatres throughout the UK, with the problem of rising costs and limited sources of finance to fund its operations. It also has its own special problems which add considerably to those it shares with other theatres, namely:-

(a)   A theatre which is large in relation to its catchment area.

(b)   Steadily declining attendances which have dropped from approximately 55% in its first year of operation to in the region of 31% in the six months to 30 September 1980.

(c)   Considerable changes to senior management during the theatre's short life which have adversely affected continuity and consistency in its operation during this time.

In our view, these problems combine to make the marketing function of the Eden Court of vital importance to its future success.

Above
Marking a turn in the financial tide, the Coopers & Lybrand Report finally convinced the funding agencies that they were not contributing enough to Eden Court Theatre.

Above
The response to their first theatre performance convinced Skye band Runrig
that they had a future beyond the Kyle of Lochalsh.

The Courier said the decision left a nasty taste in the mouth but if the theatre's financial troubles persisted, the Governors could not come back for more. "All we can now hope is that this piece of crass folly where Eden Court is concerned is the last, but we shall be very surprised indeed if that should be the case," Miss Barron added.

Following the District's decision, the Scottish Arts Council increased its grant by £27,000 to £117,000, Ross & Cromarty and Badenoch & Strathspey District Councils each decided to make an annual grant and Friends Of Eden Court cashed in £10,000 worth of its investments to make a special payment. Eden Court's slate was finally wiped clean..

Caithness District Council was unhappy about a share of the locally raised regional rate going to Eden Court when distance prevented ratepayers attending on a regular basis, however, and petitioned the Court of Session. Governors breathed another sigh of relief when the action failed.

The theatre's box office fortunes continued to be mixed, however, American country singer George Hamilton drew another full house later that month but the audiences for modern jazzman Ronnie Scott and for Scottish Opera's "outstandingly sung" "Lucia Di Lammermoor" were "woefully few", the Courier reported. Other big names in the weeks ahead were Rolf Harris, The Drifters, Mary O'Hara and Sheena Easton.

"She left the stage in tears," Val Falcon remembered. "The Eden Court audience can be very restrained and she thought they didn't like her – but they did. They just didn't show it like audiences elsewhere had done."

In April, the governors set about tackling the under-performance in the restaurant, budgeted for an £11,200 surplus on the year's workings and decided to appoint a financial manager and a marketing officer. Press officer David Carruthers was made redundant and the newly-created role

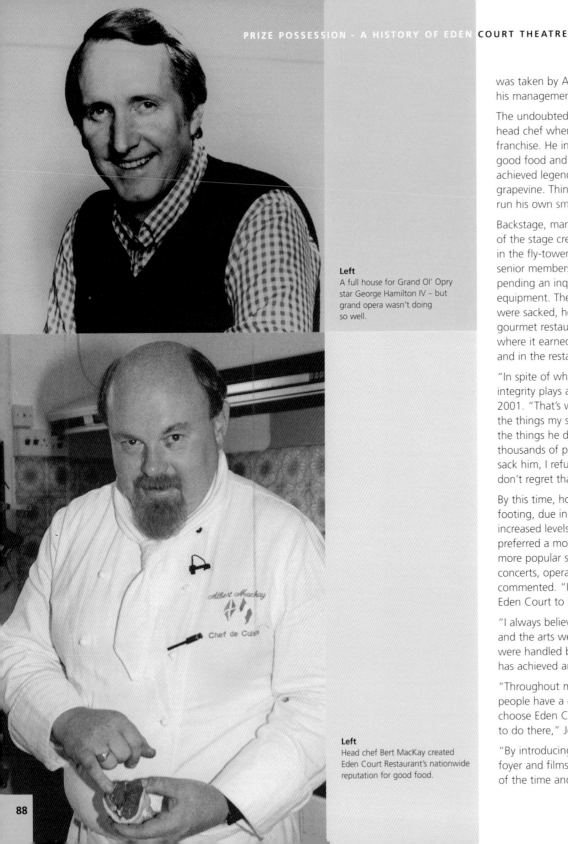

Left
A full house for Grand Ol' Opry
star George Hamilton IV – but
grand opera wasn't doing
so well.

Left
Head chef Bert MacKay created
Eden Court Restaurant's nationwide
reputation for good food.

was taken by Alan John who, like the director and many of his management team, came from the Aviemore Centre.

The undoubted success story was Bert MacKay who became head chef when the Mackenzies gave up the catering franchise. He initiated what was to become a golden age of good food and excellent service in the restaurant, which achieved legendary status on the touring performers' grapevine. Things were never quite the same after he left to run his own small hotel in the south.

Backstage, management was notoriously lax, however. One of the stage crew was reputed to have installed a bed and TV in the fly-tower and to have made his home there. Two senior members of Johnson's technical crew were suspended pending an inquiry into alleged misappropriation of theatre equipment. The director defended them and, when they were sacked, he tendered his resignation, leaving to open a gourmet restaurant first in Skye and then in rural Lancashire where it earned a regular place in "The Good Food Guide" and in the restaurant columns of many national newspapers.

"In spite of what people may or may not say about me, integrity plays a major part in my being," Johnson said in 2001. "That's why I had to leave Eden Court. I know a lot of the things my stage manager did were wrong – but a lot of the things he did were right and he saved the theatre thousands of pounds in the process and when I was told to sack him, I refused. To me it was a point of principle and I don't regret that."

By this time, however, the theatre was on a sound financial footing, due in part to Johnson's showman skills and to the increased levels of funding. "Maybe some people would have preferred a more artistic programme but if there weren't more popular shows, there wouldn't be any classical concerts, opera or ballet at all," ex-Provost Sellar commented. "It was a tight struggle but we managed to run Eden Court to budget from then on.

"I always believed the Council should provide for all interests and the arts were completely neglected. Perhaps some things were handled badly but I'm very proud of what Eden Court has achieved and my small part in it."

"Throughout my business life, I have always been aware that people have a choice and, not only did I want them to choose Eden Court, I wanted them to have a choice of what to do there," Johnson added.

"By introducing cabaret in the restaurant, discos in the stalls foyer and films in the Bishop's Palace, I tried to use as much of the time and space as I could because every minute and

PATRICIA HAY *SCOTTISH OPERA*

"'The Marriage Of Figaro'…was given in the presence of Prince Charles… he was quite 'up' on 'The Marriage Of Figaro' and said he had really enjoyed the production."

"I was vastly pregnant when I sang at Eden Court's opening concert. I was playing Pamina in Mozart's "Magic Flute" at the time and was going to sing one of her arias – but I was so large I couldn't get into the original costume. Scottish Opera had to make a voluminous pink chiffon dress to fit and disguise my condition. I came back to sing Rosina in "The Barber Of Seville" and Susanna in "The Marriage Of Figaro" which was given in the presence of Prince Charles. He spent some time with the singers after the performance and was very chatty. He was quite 'up' on "The Marriage Of Figaro" and said he had really enjoyed the production."

every square foot was costing the ratepayers money. I still think that's the right way to handle the building – although I recognise that someone with more artistic vision than me will programme it differently."

Having finally brought about a sea change in Eden Court's financial fortunes, the beleaguered governors could have expected a change in the tone of press coverage but, still smarting from five years of reading their own comments in the public prints, they decided henceforth to meet in private. "The press were honest in what they were reporting but it was always the bad side they were hearing at meetings," ex-Provost Sellar commented. "The headlines were always very critical and encouraged a lot of people to jump on the bandwagon."

The Courier called the decision midsummer madness. "It's public money upon which the theatre relies for its continued existence so there can be no denying the public's right to know how things are going at Eden Court," Miss Barron wrote. "The Press's presence not only ensures the public can be kept informed but also helps to remind all participants that they are accountable and responsible to the public."

Since then, however, the Board has met in private and managed the release of news with anodyne statements to the press – but few of them were considered worthy of printing. Real news was kept a zealously guarded secret but it usually got out, sooner or later.

CHAPTER NINE

EVERYTHING'S COMING UP ROSES

With a hitherto unreported warning that Eden Court was in danger of losing its SAC subsidy unless the arts element of the programme was increased, Catherine Robins took over from Chris Johnson in 1984. "It seemed to me that I'd just taken over a theatre that was more famous for its restaurant," she laughed. "When I told people where I was, no matter where they were, they all said: 'What a wonderful restaurant!'"

With considerable experience in drama – at Edinburgh's Theatre Workshop, at Cumbria's Rosehill Theatre and at Perth where she worked as Joan Knight's assistant, gaining further experience in administrating and directing – Robins set about correcting the programming balance, immediately boosting the drama content by booking more touring productions like the Royal Shakespeare Company's "Educating Rita" starring Tom Baker, a former "Dr Who", and the National Theatre's "Hiawatha" and by instigating her own productions which would be designed to tour the farthest-flung parts of Eden Court's catchment area.

"The idea of touring the Highlands & Islands was almost immediate and I suggested it at my interview for the job," she recalled. "I was just setting up the first tour at Perth Theatre and knowing the political difficulties Eden Court had with various councils suing Highland Region over their share of the rates going to the theatre, it seemed to me that in this job I had to do a lot of political wooing. So there was that, as well as an artistic reason, behind my proposal.

"We started with 'Para Handy' using an English writer I knew to adapt the Neil Munro stories – but I was determined to use local writers, actors and anybody with a Highland connection in future productions. I got Norman Malcolm MacDonald to write the next one, 'The Brahan Seer', and the

third, 'The Crofting Act', used various Highland writers with music provided by Donald Shaw and Karen Matheson of Capercaillie.

"I also commissioned a dramatisation of Compton MacKenzie's 'The Rival Monster' from Donald Smith and got Ian Crichton Smith to adapt Brecht's 'Wedding Party'. Caithness poet George Gunn wrote 'The Gold Of Kildonan' with music again by Donald and Karen and the last one I did was 'Atom Of Delight' – the story of Highland author Neil Gunn – written by Aonghas MacNeacail.

"I couldn't use Eden Court's main budget for the tours,' she revealed. "When I arrived I was told to cut spending by £100,000. All the touring had to be supported by local councils who were terrific, the Scottish Arts Council and private patronage."

Fresh young faces like Andy Gray and Jonathan Watson from BBC Scotland's hit TV comedy series "City Lights" were booked for the pantomimes, which Robins wrote and directed herself. She also expanded the classical music concerts, enticed Scottish Opera and Scottish Ballet into reinstating their twice-yearly visits and jumped at the chance of providing facilities for BBC TV to film concert performances by fashionable Scottish rock bands like Deacon Blue and Hue & Cry. She also booked touring productions of West End musicals like "Annie", "Gypsy", "West Side Story" and "Song And Dance" with its original stars, Marti Webb and Wayne Sleep.

In April 1986, Jimmy Logan returned as the embittered music hall comedian Archie Rice, a role made famous on stage and screen by Sir Laurence Olivier, in John Osborne's dramatic allegory, "The Entertainer". Logan's name and the play's title led some of the Eden Court audience to expect a family

Left
Persistence paid off when impresario Cameron Mackintosh brought his West End hit, "Five Guys Named Moe" to Eden Court in 1995.

Left
Catherine Robins took over as
director in 1984 and, by reviving
the touring theatre company, took
Eden Court to places it hadn't
reached in five years.

Above
The Royal Shakespeare Company
made its Eden Court debut at
Eden Court with "Educating Rita"
starring TV's "Dr Who", Tom Baker.

comedy. "Reaction was mixed," Logan recalled. "
One woman said she'd spent a better night with
the toothache.

"It was a challenge – for me and for the audience. They had
to get used to seeing me in an entirely different role and in a
'play theatre' like The Byre, St Andrew's, the response
was terrific."

"My policy for the first two years was to put on something
for everybody and make the building open to all,"
Robins said. "We had Saturday morning music, children's
entertainments, workshops and good quality touring drama
and music. Again, the whole purpose behind it – and this
was fairly unique at the time – was to build up a relationship
with the companies and make sure they came back."
Both the RSC and the National Theatre were to return with
"Dangerous Liaisons" and "The Visit".

Robins presided over Eden Court's tenth anniversary in 1986
with a number of special events spread throughout the year.
She also recognised that the main auditorium was too large
for certain performances and, in conjunction with Inverness
District Council conference officer, Caroline Munro, she
launched an initiative to provide an exhibition hall that would
double as a performance space for amateur and small-scale
touring productions.

At that time Eden Court was attracting major events like the
European Parliament's LOHME Convention and the EC's
Cartoon Forum, which required marquees to be erected on
the theatre lawns. Finance for a permanent building was not
available – but, with funding from the Scottish Film Council
and £23,000 from Friends of Eden Court, Robins was able to
realise her predecessor's vision of converting the makeshift
cinema in the Bishop's Palace into a state-of-the-art
mini cinema.

Following the opening of Riverside Screen, the Scottish Film
Council – which had launched "Movie Makars", an annual
seminar for aspiring screen-writers, producers and directors,
in 1990 – moved it to Eden Court. Under the patronage of
Council chairman and screen writer Alan Shiach – who
moonlighted as the chairman of The MacAllan Distillery – it
has attracted many of the film world's top names like the
Oscar-winning William Goldman, writer of "Butch Cassidy
And The Sundance Kid", and Nicholas Roeg, director of the
classic supernatural thriller "Don't Look Now" starring Julie
Christie and Donald Sutherland. The film "Trainspotting"
emerged from "Movie Makars" and producer Douglas Boyd
presented the Oscar-nominated "Mrs Brown" with Judi
Dench and Billy Connolly as a case study before its
commercial release.

Right
Oscar-winning screen-writer
William Goldman was one of the
top Hollywood names who offered
their knowledge and experience to
help Scotland's aspiring screen-
writers at "Movie Makars".

Left
Creating stars of Scottish
panto - Andy Gray and
Jonathon Watson appeared
in Catherine Robin's
production of "Sinbad".

EDEN COURT-ON TOUR

THE GOLD OF KILDONAN

A NEW PLAY BY
GEORGE GUNN

EDEN COURT THEATRE

THE BRAHAN SEER

A NEW PLAY BY
NORMAN MALCOLM MACDONALD

Mon 29th Sept - Sat 4th Oct
7.45 pm nightly
Tickets £5.00
Concession £3.50 (Mon - Thur only)
BOX OFFICE Tel: (0463) 221718

Left
A series of posters from the Touring Company set up by Catherine Robins.

Right
Education Officer Sonia Rose and her team of Starféis workers spearheaded Eden Court's cause in schools throughout the Highlands.

Widely regarded as the strongest and most effective support organisation of its kind, Friends of Eden Court raised over £350,000 for Eden Court in 25 years. The £10,000 lifeline in 1981 was the biggest donation until that time but – as with its contribution to Riverside Screen – the annual contribution often exceeded that sum in subsequent years.

"Encouraging young people to take an interest in the theatre has been another of our primary concerns all the way along and we ran workshops until Sonia Rose was appointed as the theatre's education officer in 1990," Friends fourth and longest-serving organiser Rona Kirk added.

A former art teacher at Charleston Academy, Rose is paid by Highland Council's Education Department and based at the theatre. She organises music, drama and dance workshops and performances in schools throughout the Highland Region and produces her own touring shows with the help of Friends Of Eden Court, notably "Ready Or Not" which was set in a 19th century Highland classroom and was specially written by Caithness-born writer James Miller.

Up until 2001, the education officer raised £940,000 in grants from outside sources to support and develop her work, including the four-year Starféis programme financed by the Esmée Fairburn Foundation which enabled her to appoint

drama workers in Caithness, Skye, Lochaber, Ross-shire and Badenoch, Strathspey & Nairn and culminated in the Skye youth theatre group winning through to the national finals of the BT Connections drama competition in the National Theatre in London.

Starféis was followed by the two-years ACTivators programme set up in 2000 with grant from the SAC-administered National Lottery Fund, the "After School Arts Project", financed by the National Lottery's New Opportunities Fund, and "Out Of Eden", an Eden Court initiative funded by various trusts and foundations.

"My function is to promote interest and participation in the theatre among young people, enabling them to develop their social and personal skills and acquire an awareness and appreciation of the arts," Rose said. "The activities also provide Eden Court with the opportunity of offering a service to young people in small communities outwith Inverness who might not be able to come to the theatre very often."

Rose initiated "Rhythms Of the North", the theatre's annual showcase for musical talent in Highland schools – but young performers had access to the theatre's stage from the outset when Murray Edwards tapped into the International Festival Of Youth Orchestras in Aberdeen. Highland Regional Council launched its own biennial international youth festival of music and dance in the 1980s, holding gala concerts in the theatre which also hosts the annual competitive Inverness Music Festival and showcases for the féisean movement, a Gaelic initiative to coach young people in music, song, drama and dance.

In her final year at Eden Court, Robins created the post of drama worker in residence and Kieran Gillespie was subsequently appointed. His activities included a youth production of "The Elephant Man". When his contract ended, John Batty who went on to develop more projects for people of all ages and abilities succeeded him.

With "Top City", an organisation set up to raise Inverness's national profile and prestige, Robins proposed an arts festival – but she had moved on by the time the idea was adopted and evolved into the Highland Festival which staged its flagship events at Eden Court.

Above
The last Chairman of the Highlands and Islands Development Board, driving force behind the HI-Light Year Of The Arts and a member of the Theatre's Board of Governors, Sir Robert Cowan.

Unlike those of her predecessors, Robins' years as director were not dogged by financial crisis. "The biggest controversy I had was probably over the screening of Martin Scorsese's "The Last Temptation Of Christ" which attracted a lot of protest from religious groups and which the Council banned without seeing," she recalled. "I remember one minister who objected telling me he was really upset about the ban because he'd have liked to see the film!"

Robins had a more relaxed attitude to the press and, assisted by a strong management team which included Inverness District Council's former assistant director of finance Roger Niven, later succeeded by the job-sharing Gill Cooper and Simon Tomsett, and John Petchey, Lisa Fuchs and David Smith in the marketing and publicity department, the theatre obtained much favourable and constructive coverage in the media.

The situation was assisted by a change in ownership of the Courier, who introduced an arts page. The Highland News and later The Press & Journal followed suit and Highland Board chairman, the late Sir Robert Cowan, who had succeeded Robert Fasken on the theatre's Board of Governors and spearheaded the HIDB's innovative Year Of The Arts in 1991 – forerunner of the Highland Festival of which his widow, Margaret, was founding chairman – maintained the coverage had a beneficial effect on Eden Court's box office.

One problem that had defeated her predecessors continued to defy Robins, however. Theatre attendances dipped during the bright nights and a summer season was unprofitable. She tried spectaculars with big names like Bob Monkhouse and traditional Scottish variety shows in the restaurant but could not compete with the rival "Summer Showtime".

In 2001, based in Halifax, West Yorkshire, and working as a consultant to other theatres, she still hadn't found an answer. "In England, there's not such a big contrast in light but it's still a problem, "Robins said. "People just don't want to stay indoors on summer nights."

Her marketing director, who was appointed In February 1987, had previously worked with English National Opera and Robins made him responsible for planning the theatre's music programme. John Petchey devised the international concert season of ten concerts, which was launched in 1990 with the Bolshoi Orchestra.

Conducted by its music director Alexander Lazarev, later to become chief conductor of the Royal Scottish National Orchestra, the orchestra of Moscow's famous ballet and opera theatre made only one other Scottish appearance –

Above
Caithness born author James Miller has written plays for Eden Court and 'The Magic Curtain', a short history of theatre in Inverness published by the Friends of Eden Court.

Above
Bob Monkhouse was one of the stars of the Sunday Spectacular series but it still failed to draw summer audiences.

Above
After his 1990 appearance with
The Bolshoi Orchestra, Alexander
Lazarev was to return to Eden
Court as principal conductor of the
Royal Scottish National Orchestra.

in Glasgow during the city's reign as European Capital of Culture. The following year, the season's international dimension was furnished by the Bergen Philharmonic, with Inverness born George Silver from India Street in the trumpet section.

Russian-born Maxim Venegerov inherited the mantle of Heifitz and Menuhin as one of the world's great violin virtuosos – but on 9th October 1991, one of the first Western audiences to appreciate his talent was at Eden Court for his appearance with the RSNO under Lazarev. Viola virtuoso Yuri Bashmet was another charismatic soloist acquiring an international stature when he first appeared at Eden Court with the Moscow Soloists on 19th October 1988. He was later to return with the Scottish Chamber Orchestra in March 1996.

With the fall of the Berlin Wall and the collapse of communism, an increasing number of East European orchestras were able to tour in the West and anxious to increase their income. Russian, Polish and East German orchestras gave four of the twelve concerts the following season. Lazarev and the Bolshoi, the Moscow State Symphony and the Polish National Radio Orchestras returned the following year – but of course the East European Orchestras were not the only international element in the programmes.

The soloists and conductors came from all over the world, not only Venegerov and Bashmet but also the Spanish pianist Alicia de Larrocha, the young German violinist Franz Peter Zimmerman, the veteran Russian-born pianist Shura Cherkassky, the Polish conductor composer Krzystof Penderecki and Viennese-born Walter Weller, not to mention Ulsterman James Galway, England's Julian Lloyd Webber and Scotland's own Evelyn Glennie. Regrettably, the Viennese-born piano virtuoso Alfred Brendel had to cancel his appearance with the SCO because of an elbow injury.

"I was sorry we never got Brendel but I'm very proud of having brought people like Venegerov, Lazarev and Bashmet to Eden Court," Petchey commented. "It put us on the map internationally. Performers went back to their agents and said they'd had a wonderful time, we got good press and it was good marketing. The East European orchestras were desperate to travel and earn sterling and, equally, they were able to increase our attendances at concerts."

Another big draw was the iconoclastic violin virtuoso Nigel Kennedy whose punk clothes had nothing on the outfit he found at Eden Court. After his performance, usherettes showed him round the theatre and when he got to the

Above
The young Russian violin virtuoso Maxim Venegerov made one of his earliest British appearances at Eden Court and is now a major international attraction.

Right
There is nothing like a Dame as
Nigel Kennedy tries on a panto
outfit – outrageous even by his
standards – after a 1991
appearance at Eden Court.

wardrobe department, he persuaded Moira Bromley Wiggins,
who was at work on costumes for the forthcoming panto, to
let him dress up as dame.

Of the West End musicals that began to visit Eden Court,
perhaps the greatest coup was attracting Cameron
Mackintosh's hit production, "Five Guys Named Moe" to the
Highland theatre in February 1995.

"I'd been to see 'Les Miserables' and said to Catherine:
'We've got to get something like that'," Petchey recalled. "I
wanted 'Cats' but Cameron Mackintosh's office specified a
minimum nine-week run which was impossible for us. 'Les
Mis' was too big for our stage, they said, and I wrote back
and said it wasn't. We had the biggest stage in Scotland and
I suggested he come and see for himself. That's when he said
he was willing to put on 'Five Guys Named Moe' and would
come up and talk to us all."

By the time the show was staged – with the soon-to-be-
knighted Mackintosh himself in attendance – Catherine
Robins had left to take up an appointment as administrator
of Northern Theatre Ballet in Yorkshire.

Proposals for Kenneth Branagh and Emma Thompson also
caused a stir in the theatre. At the suggestion of Thompson's
mother, Scots actress Phyllida Law, a frequent Highland visitor
and Friend of Eden Court, Branagh planned to direct
Thompson in a reworking of "Hedda Gabler", rehearsing and
opening the show in Inverness before taking it to London –
but there were problems with the script and the project had
to be abandoned.

Above
In 1991 Inverness-born trumpeter George Silver, a former member of the
Scottish National Orchestra, returned to his birthplace with the Bergen
Philharmonic Orchestra, once conducted by Grieg, himself the descendant of
a Scots exile.

bove
iend of Eden Court, Phyllida Law
ersuaded daughter Emma
hompson (together in a scene
om the film "The Winter Guest")
 prepare "Hedda Gabler" at
den Court.

One of the most popular plays staged at Eden Court at this time was a touring production of the acclaimed Irish drama, "Dancing at Lughnasa", starring the versatile Dillie Keane from the cabaret team Fascinating Aïda. The final night of the run has gone down in theatre folklore.

"The safety curtain was lowered at the interval and, try as they might, the stage crew just couldn't raise it again," Val Falcon remembered. "This was the best-attended play we'd ever had and it was an absolute disaster that the show couldn't go on. I made an announcement from one of the boxes to tell the audience what had happened and went backstage to see what could be done.

"I knew Dillie from her previous visits with Fascinating Aïda and she got the cast to go into the box and finish off the story from there. They got a terrific round of applause for doing that – and, because John Petchey and James Shaw Grant were at the performance and took the decision, I was able to tell the audience that partial refunds would be made.

"I was an absolute wreck – and when I tell the story at house-management courses, it always wins first prize for the worst thing that has ever happened to a house manager!"

Right
The safety curtain started acting up again in 1995 and deprived the Saturday evening audience of the last act of "Dancing At Lughnasa".

After a brief inter-regnum when the theatre was run by her management team, Robins' successor, Paul Maurel, took up his appointment in 1994. Both his parents had been opera singers but his theatrical inclinations lay in administration and he had gained experience directing theatres in Gainsborough and Belfast where he had a proven record in raising funds for development.

At Eden Court, he ended the theatre's practice of "in-house" panto production and brought in a contracting company, which relied on TV soap stars instead of familiar Scottish performers which audiences had come to expect – a move unpopular with older panto patrons whose custom was considered vital to the show's box office returns.

Maurel also favoured state-funded companies like the Red Army Ensemble, the Georgian State Dancers, the Chinese State Circus, Kodo drummers from Japan and dance troupes from Africa and India which introduced Eden Court's audiences to new cultural experiences – and were less costly than the big West End Shows favoured by Robins.

Repairs and maintenance, so often shelved in the past for financial reasons, had now become a matter of urgency. At a performance by the Royal Marines Band, a leaking roof dampened the enthusiasm of those sitting in the front rows of the stalls. The programme, appropriately included an arrangement of Handel's "Water Music"!

The Governors set up a fund-raising committee and Maurel was asked to draw up an application for funds from the newly-established National Lottery which awarded some of its profits to capital projects in the arts. To ensure sympathy with the theatre's original design, the plans were devised at Law & Dunbar-Nasmith by architect Colin Ross, working to the late Graham Law's original drawings. The bid was successful and led to an impressive £1.2m refurbishment of the theatre auditorium and improved access for the disabled.

Soon after Maurel's appointment, however, it became clear there were strains between him and his marketing director who was eventually suspended for issuing complimentary tickets for the fourth annual appearance by The Russian Ice Stars without Maurel's authority. Petchey maintained the tickets had come from the promoter's allocation and were distributed on her instructions. The Board backed its director and Petchey was sacked.

The chairman and vice-chairman, ex-Provost William Fraser and James Shaw Grant, insisted to the press that the decision was the right one, but four governors – Jean Urquhart and Regional Councillors Bryan Beattie, Janet MacInnes and Molly

Right
Paul Maurel, who took over in 1995, put together the successful fund–raising application that gave the interior of Eden Court a smart new look.

Above
During Maurel's stewardship, Eden Court brought the world to Eden Court's doorstep with spectacular attractions from Vienna, Georgia and China.

Doyle – remained convinced that the marketing director had got a raw deal.

Disquieted by Maurel's actions, their concern increased when the Countess of Cromarty resigned from Eden Court's fund-raising committee after an exchange with the theatre director whose manner also upset the most powerful man in British theatre, Cameron Mackintosh, when the impresario brought "Five Guys Named Moe" to Eden Court.

Petchey went to an Industrial Tribunal and the panel decided he had been unfairly dismissed – but found his actions had been a contributing factor and did not order his reinstatement. He was subsequently invited to become a Scottish Arts Council assessor of grant-assisted events, which took him back to Eden Court in an official capacity.

Other staff departed amid considerable publicity – with a consequent effect on the morale of those who remained – and in January 1997, the Courier demanded: "What is going on at Eden Court?"

With the re-organisation of local government and the dissolution of district councils in May 1996, the new Highland Council became entirely responsible for Eden Court and a new Board was appointed under the chairmanship of Councillor Beattie, chairman of the new authority's Culture & Leisure Services Committee and formerly Arts Development Officer for Stirling and Ross & Cromarty District Council. It took a much more critical attitude towards the theatre director's performance.

The number of "dark" nights and film presentations in the main auditorium increased as the director grappled with cuts in funding arising from the abolition of district councils and the creation of a unitary authority.

Faced with its mounting losses, Maurel had closed the theatre's restaurant and started planning to convert it into a studio theatre. Trial performances were held but, by this time, the new Board was alarmed that the deficit was now threatening the theatre's future. After sixteen years of stability, the past had returned to haunt the present Governors; Eden Court was back on the financial rocks.

"The Board asked the director for a report on ways of clearing the deficit and after discussion they voted for the option to effectively close Eden Court for six months," Beattie recalled. "I couldn't accept that, so I asked the Arts Council and Highland Council for guarantees that they wouldn't let the theatre go under and called an extraordinary general meeting to get the decision rescinded.

"It was a fairly seminal moment… definitely touch and go," the Board chairman declared. "Eden Court came within an ace of closing its doors and there was no way anyone who would even consider that could remain as director. That was not what he was there for. We therefore decided not to renew his contract."

But not before Maurel's supporters on the sharply divided Board, valuing his business sense, tried unsuccessfully to strike a compromise by proposing a year's extension of the director's contract and setting him financial targets. Beattie's supporters, however, were in the majority.

Maurel was succeeded in September 1997 by Colin Marr who had previously held management posts at The Queen's Hall and the Traverse Theatre where he had gained not only experience in theatre administration but in music and drama programming. He needed both – because when he examined the books, the theatre was in deeper trouble than he expected.

"It was frightening," he recalled. "Not only was there a cumulative deficit from previous years of around £130,000 but that year's operating was heading for a £54,000 deficit. The theatre had a good financial year in 95/96 but, as a result of local government reorganisation, the theatre's grant had been cut by £100,000 that year and £50,000 the following year. It seemed very little adjustment had been made to take account of these cuts.

"I'd had a couple of days with Paul Maurel before I started and on my first day I met most of the staff. The finance

Above
When Colin Marr took over as
director in 1997, his first task was
clearing the deficit he had inherited
from his predececessor.

officer, Archie MacTaggart, set up a meeting with the auditors who hadn't signed away the previous year's accounts. They explained that they would have to qualify them as saying the theatre wasn't a going concern. That sort of statement makes people call in the money owed to them and things then go horribly wrong.

"They agreed to sign them off after seeing a financial plan to clear the deficit and I had until December to come up with one. I made it with two days to spare and we managed to finish that year in surplus rather than deficit. The theatre had no programme past Christmas but the one I came up with made some money. Otherwise, I just didn't let anyone spend anything!"

Marr also resumed full responsibility for programming and financial control – functions delegated by his predecessor – and the two consequent redundancies helped him reduce the deficit even further.

Having concluded that the theatre's programme lacked variety and pandered slightly towards the elite, he set about restoring a balance. "It seemed Eden Court was considered to be a No 1 theatre – whatever that means – and would only take No. 1 product. Fine, but that often involves large fees and long runs and we don't have the population to sustain that, so I took a very simple approach of trying to fill everyone's needs, trying to get as much variety as possible.

"Running a theatre is a strange job because your own tastes have to be completely buried," he added. "It's not about what I like, it's about what our patrons like, so I spoke to people as much as I could. There was no methodology in it; we didn't get round to a proper survey until last year."

In an interview with the Inverness Courier, he appealed to readers to let him know what they wanted – and they did.

"With grants of £211,000 from the Arts Council and £500,000 from Highland Council, the theatre is subsidised to the tune of about £2 per head of population – but the programme has to make money overall which is not something I think it ever did before," Marr explained. "£50-60,000 a year is required which is not a massive amount on a box office turnover of over £1,000,000 but there's a limit to what people will pay for tickets. You've got to allow them access at a price they can afford – which probably applies more to opera than Daniel O'Donnell.

Above
Rebuilding the theatre programme,
Colin Marr obtained additional funds
to reintroduce contemporary dance.

"I don't particularly believe in the elitist argument but I'm aware it's there and it's something we have to be careful to counter. Ballet and opera is not for a certain section of society, it's for people who like ballet and opera – and they are by no means the bow-tie and ball-gown set."

Marr favoured Scottish and, more particularly, Highland product of quality. "We have a responsibility to connect the Highlands to the mainstream of Scottish arts activity, so I re-established all our links with the Scottish companies, including the smaller-scale ones. I'm well aware they aren't to everyone's taste and they're too small for our stage and auditorium but, until we have a studio theatre, I don't think we should be deprived of seeing them."

With the co-operation of a board chaired for the first time by an arts professional, Marr not only increased the level of programming, boosting the drama content with regular visits by Borderline, 7:84 and Dundee Rep., he negotiated a higher level of participation by Scottish orchestras in the international concert series and set about arranging bi-annual visits by Scottish Opera and Scottish Ballet. He also obtained extra cash to promote contemporary dance and because many of the performances were of medium scale and therefore medium cost, he soon wiped out the cumulative deficit he had inherited.

With a rise in staff morale, audience satisfaction and Board confidence came an increase in box office income – which stood the theatre in good stead when in 1999/2000, the Scottish Arts Council awarded a standstill grant and followed it the following year with a slight increase that barely covered the two years' inflation.

Gradually, however, Marr found he was able to book more of the "blockbuster" events that Eden Court's audiences had come to expect and, as the theatre's 25th anniversary approached, he revived the plan to create a custom-built studio theatre meeting the needs of local amateurs and small-scale touring companies, as envisaged in John Wyckham's original plan. The outline application for Lottery funding also covered a major redevelopment of the now-outdated building.

"I'm well aware of how building costs can rise, particularly with regard to Eden Court," he told the Courier. "The builders and architects have quoted £4m – but I'm budgeting for £5m."

Successfully passing through every stage of the Scottish Arts Council's vetting process can take 18 months to three years to obtain final approval but Marr clearly wants

Far left
Eden Court celebrated its 25th anniversary with the first in a wide-ranging series of concerts which was given by Scottish Opera under its musical director Richard Armstrong who had made his Eden Court debut the evening before at a performance of "Don Giovanni".

Left
Colin Marr obtained additional funds to ensure the continuation of a programme of jazz concerts.

to avoid the mistakes of the past and he looks to the future with cautious confidence and optimism.

On Saturday 21st April 2001 – the closest he could get to the actual 25th anniversary of the official opening – Marr staged a celebration concert featuring the orchestra, chorus and soloists of Scottish Opera conducted by its musical director, Richard Armstrong, who had made his Eden Court debut at a performance of Mozart's "Don Giovanni" the previous evening. It was one of a series of special events held throughout the year and two of them marked other 25th anniversaries. Phil Cunningham celebrated quarter of a century in show-business by appearing in concert with some of his musical friends and Inverness Jazz Platform, which had been helped through funding difficulties by Colin Marr, commemorated its 25th birthday with a "Centenary Salute To Louis Armstrong" which was broadcast by BBC Radio 3 and featured top American, English and Scottish performers.

Over the past 25 years, every director has contributed in his or her own way to developing Eden Court and enhancing its position as the premier arts venue in the Highlands and a major player on the Scottish theatre circuit, continuing to attract audiences from throughout the region to a wide variety of events and fulfilling the dream of the last Inverness Town Council.

Murray Edwards opened the theatre and established its reputation with audiences, performers and promoters. With the assistance of increased grants, Chris Johnson made Eden Court accessible to a wider public, set it on an even financial keel and introduced the second screen concept.

Catherine Robins strengthened Eden Court's drama programme, re-establishing the theatre's touring activities, extending Eden Court's presence throughout the Highlands and Islands, introduced a regime of monthly classical concerts and turned Chris Johnson's Highlands & Islands Film Guild operation into the fully furnished Riverside Screen.

Paul Maurel, who went to run two theatres in Surrey which have now closed and could not be traced during the preparation of this book, brought the world to Eden Court audiences and put together the successful funding application that enabled a major and long-overdue refurbishment of the theatre to take place.

Apart from those already mentioned, many other illustrious performers have beguiled Eden Court audiences over the years —from major classical recording artists like Korean violin virtuoso Kyung Wha Chung, the brilliant Japanese pianist Mitsuko Uchida, the great French flautist Jean-Pierre Rampal, the poetic Portuguese pianist Joao Maria Pirès and the dynamic French piano duo Katia and Maria Labeque.

Top comedy acts like Ken Dodd, Jim Davidson, Ben Elton, Rik Mayall, Lenny Henry, Eddie Izzard, Paul Merton and musical comedy star Gary Wilmot, distinguished actors like Judi Dench, Sian Phillips, Susan Hampshire, Richard Todd and Scotland's own Tom Fleming and David MacCallum, The Royal Ballet's prima ballerina Darcey Bussell, and Country superstars like Tammy Wynette, Don Williams, Crystal Gayle and Charley Pride have all appeared at Eden Court, as have major inaternational TV and recording artists Nana Mouskouri, The Dubliners, Clannad and Daniel O'Donnell, David Essex, the BBC Big Band, top jazz artists Monty Alexander, Carol Kidd and Scott Hamilton and leading Scottish bands like The Proclaimers, Capercaillie and the Highlands' own Wolfstone who, like Runrig, launched their stage career at the Inverness theatre.

Above
Wolfstone

Left and above
Eddie Izzard, Darcey Bussell, David Essex and the Highlands' own
Wolfstone – among the big names that Eden Court has brought to
Inverness in recent years.

Above
Eden Court's conference facilities
have brought added value to
Inverness over the years.

Cost, distance and auditorium size – still considerable factors in determining Eden Court's programme – may have caused such glittering occasions to be few and far between but that only served to make them all the more special

Against the expectations of the Jeremiahs, the theatre has overcome the often daunting setbacks that dogged its conception, construction and early operation, becoming an institution that has enriched and expanded the experience of living in the Highlands, triumphantly fulfilling the hopes of those who had championed its cause in adverse times.

The original concept of a civic complex for conferences, drama and music was Provost Mackay's. Provost Smith identified the site but it was amateur performer Jimmy Pringle who re-asserted the need for a proper theatre, a concept enthusiastically shared and pursued by Douglas Baxter with the powerful backing of Provost Smith who recognised that Eden Court would enhance the status of the town and of Councillor Nicolson who swung the Region behind the project

There seems little doubt that Provost Smith and Treasurer Fraser would not have urged the Council to accept the £1.3 tender if it had not been for the guidance of Town Clerk John R. Hill and Town Chamberlain Derek Bigg. Later Treasurer Fraser and Provost Sellar staked their political reputations to bring Eden Court through a severe financial crisis in running costs, even Provost Ian Fraser kept the faith in characteristically laconic style – and Inverness District Council overcame acute misgivings, prejudice and hostility to deliver crucial funds at critical times and in challenging circumstances.

Voices against the theatre are no longer raised. Ewan MacQueen died in 1983, seven years after the theatre opened, and although Eden Court has been used regularly by religious denominations, notably for Easter worship and by the National Bible Society's Prom Praise, his daughter is sure he would not have moderated his views. "My father was a man of conviction," Inverness primary schoolteacher Eona MacQueen said. "His objections were on financial as well as religious grounds."

Andrew MacDonald went to work on the Continent and is now living in Boulogne and Miss Barron, who subsequently reviewed many of the performances staged at Eden Court even as she maintained her unrelenting objections to the size and cost of the building, died in 1990. Often asked how she reconciled her attendance at the theatre with her vociferous opposition to it, she would snap:

Above
Labour leader John Smith addresses the party's Scottish conference at Eden Court. His death was announced at a Conservative Party conference at the same venue by a tearful Ian Lang, a former Secretary of State for Scotland.

Above
Celebrating Eden Court's 25th birthday in April 2001, the theatre's first Director Murray Edwards (right), and the current Director Colin Marr toast the future.

"WHAT EDEN COURT COURT MEANS TO ME"

HUMPHREY LYTTELTON

"I thought Eden Court was one of the finest venues we'd played in."

On our first visit to Inverness, we didn't want to risk damaging our double bass by putting it in the hold, so British Airways said we had to book a seat for it – which seemed ridiculous when the plane wasn't full. When a local newspaper ran the story, we were able to borrow one locally. I thought Eden Court was one of the finest venues we'd played in, so I was astonished to find out in the hotel bar after the show that many local people didn't like it because it cost so much – not the first time we've come across that reaction to a new venue – but I'm delighted that it's thriving. A happy ending to both stories!

"I was opposed to the scale and cost of it; I was never opposed to what would go on inside it."

With the benefit of the longest and closest involvement with Eden Court, first as a member and latterly Burgh Treasurer on Inverness Town Council, as a member and provost of Inverness District Council and as a member and chairman of the theatre's Board Of Governors, ex-Provost William Fraser looks back on his part with satisfaction.

"By the time I finished on the Council in 1996, the theatre was in quite a healthy state and although it did have some problems since then, they're all behind it again and it's on an even keel once more," he said.

"There's no doubt the Council recognised the value of Eden Court – not just as a theatre but as a conference centre and the cost of our annual promotional visit to London was money well spent," he added. "It was reckoned a sizeable conference used to bring £300,000 into the town and the promotional budget was recovered many times over.

"Those attended by prime ministers and party leaders got nationwide TV coverage and Princess Anne put Eden Court on the world map when she attended an international medical conference.

"The Queen and Prince Charles came to the theatre on separate occasions to present the Highland Business Awards and, on their first official visit to Inverness, the Duke and Duchess of York attended a gala performance by Scottish Opera – and, of course, the Queen Mother contributed to the Eden Court Appeal."

"White Elephant" was the epithet most often applied by Eden Court's opponents in its early days – but time has proved they were wrong and the late Rev. Murdo Nicolson was right.

Over the years, thousands of people – of all ages and from all parts of the Highlands and Islands – have had their spirits uplifted and their attitudes enlightened by the diversity and quality of the performances in their regional theatre. To them, Eden Court is indeed a prize possession.

CHAPTER TEN

THE NEXT 25 YEARS...
AND BEYOND

Playing a key part in Highland development

Dr James Hunter
Chairman, Highlands & Islands Enterprise

When, in the early 1970s, the late Provost William Smith made it clear that he was determined to press ahead with the construction of Eden Court, a great deal of criticism came his way. Ostensibly this criticism was on the grounds of cost but, underlying it, I feel, was something much more fundamental – a widespread reluctance to embrace the possibility that the northern part of Scotland should aspire to leadership in the arts or in anything else.

Matters were not always so. Go to Trinity College Library, Dublin, and you'll see there, in the shape of The Book of Kells, one of the greatest artistic achievements of Europe's early Middle Ages. This most spectacular of illuminated gospels was produced in the Highlands and Islands – at the monastery of Iona which was then one of our continent's principle centres of learning and high culture.

Nor was the Iona achievement in any way unique. The later medieval Lordship of The Isles, centred principally on Islay and Dingwall, may not have produced art on a par with that to be seen in The Book of Kells but its sculptured tombs and its surviving Gaelic poetry are enduring testimony to the importance attached in the Lordship to creativity of every kind.

Left
Dr James Hunter, Chairman of Highlands & Islands Enterprise foresees Eden Court continuing to play a vital part in his agency's strategy for Highland Development.

Far left
Giving credibility to Celtic music – Mary Anne Kennedy confronted other contemporary Highland composers with the Gaelic psalm-singing tradition and challenged them to write for the combined forces of vocal and instrumental group Cliar and massed choirs. The result was the award-winning "Lasair Dhé – The Flame Of God" – performed at Eden Court during the 1999 Highland Festival.

What was true of The Lordship of The Isles was equally true of its northern equivalent, the Earldom of Orkney. Kirkwall's Cathedral of St Magnus, an accomplishment of the Earldom, is without parallel in Scotland and is one of the most impressive medieval churches in all the British Isles.

The people responsible for The Book of Kells or the Cathedral of St Magnus were not people who thought of themselves or their religion as marginal, peripheral, remote. They believed themselves to be at the centre of things and their art reflects their tremendous self-confidence.

In more recent centuries, however, this self-confidence was lost right across the Highlands and Islands. As our area was absorbed, first into the Scottish state and, second, into the United Kingdom, political and other forms of authority were steadily drained southwards. Then came The Clearances, mass emigration and all the rest. We were left, in the middle years of the 20th Century, with a steadily contracting economy and a falling population. It is understandable, in such circumstances, that optimism should have been lacking; it is understandable that success, in a Highlands and Islands context, should have become more or less synonymous with taking yourself off to the Lowlands, to England, to the United States, Canada or Australia.

Today's Highlands and Islands, in contrast, are on the way back, the way up. Over the last 20 or 30 years, a period when the population of Scotland as a whole has been static at best, the population of the Highlands and Islands has increased by nearly 20%. During the same period, the number of people in work in the Highlands and Islands has gone up by nearly 50%.

Is it simply accidental that the turning point in our region's fortunes coincided with the decision – taken, as noted at the outset, in the face of much hostility – to press ahead with Eden Court? Definitely not. While all sorts of factors have contributed to the current resurgence of the Highlands and Islands, a key role has been played by the arts in all their forms.

Developing a region economically is not just a matter of building advanced factories or encouraging inward investment – though these things are, of course, important. If you want a depressed locality to have improved economic prospects, you have to make its people feel better about themselves. And that's where the arts can make a huge contribution. If a locality's people feel that cultural accomplishment is, almost by definition, something that happens somewhere else, then the locality in question is unlikely to be successful. It will forever be content with what's

derivative, what's second-best

Eden Court has been about boosting the self-confidence of the Highlands and Islands in general, and of Inverness in particular. But for all that it's helped greatly with this task, it's a task which has by no means been completed. Propose a University of the Highlands and Islands, suggest that Inverness and the wider Highlands might be nominated as Europe's capital of culture and you immediately encounter the same sort of scepticism and hostility which confronted Eden Court's founders and promoters.

We need finally to put all such self-doubt behind us. Scenically and environmentally, the Highlands and Islands are one of the most outstandingly attractive parts of Europe. Developments in information technology, telecommunications and the like are making it possible for us to develop here the sorts of businesses and industries that would once have had to be located in southern urban centres. There's absolutely no reason therefore, why we should not be aspiring to make the Highlands and Islands – on the back of both their natural heritage and the new enterprises becoming feasible – one of the most flourishing, most dynamic areas in Britain.

But if we're to set ourselves that goal – and if we're to achieve it – we need to build on the Eden Court experience. We need to create a climate of opinion that makes it natural for people here to aspire to be at the forefront – culturally and artistically as well as every other way. The creators of The Book Of Kells took that sort of thinking for granted. We do not. For all that's been achieved in Inverness and in the wider Highlands and Islands over the last 25 years, far too many folk hereabouts still can't quite bring themselves to believe our region's huge potential.

That's why it's so good to be able to point to Eden Court. All the numerous moaners and groaners who said that Inverness shouldn't aspire to have a first-rate theatre because such a theatre would be too expensive and couldn't possibly succeed, can now be seen to have been hopelessly and totally wrong. If we commit ourselves to providing the Highlands and Islands with a good university, to making this area Europe's capital of culture, to providing our region with a first-rate economy, then all the many folk who habitually pour cold water on those aspirations will one day be shown to have been every bit as much in error as the original critics of Eden Court.

Preparing to face new artistic and technical challenges

Bryan Beattie
Chairman of Eden Court's
Board of Governors.

Reminding people of the impact Eden Court makes on Inverness and the Highlands and Islands is an ongoing job, and not one that always wins receptive ears. But the truth of it is that the theatre succeeds on a number of levels.

• Culturally, it provides unique facilities for the area. It acts as a stimulus and a platform for local artists, an outlet and inroad to a new audience for visiting companies, and a provider of fine things for its audience.

• Socially, it is a gathering point for a hugely diverse range of social groups. Visit on a night when an orchestra is playing, or when Daniel O' Donnell is in town, or when the Ceol nam Féis kids take over the building and you'll see how many people claim ownership of the building and feel comfortable in it.

• Economically, it is a lifeline for over 100 members of part-time and full-time staff, as well as injecting over £2m into the local economy each year with the consequent employment impact that entails.

• Emotionally, it is the first point of contact for many people with a broad range of sensual and intellectual experiences through classes and outreach workshops as well as performances.

• Educationally, it continues to provide opportunities in and out of the building for people of all ages and abilities to participate in a range of artforms and performances.

Yet even after 25 years there are still some who are unaware of this breadth of impact. The theatre is something the Highlands should be immensely proud of, and vaunt, and take advantage of. It is a cultural beacon for the Highlands and Islands and, of course, for Inverness. It has a responsibility to the people of the area, as well as the funding bodies, to maximise its potential.

In the next 25 years the theatre must take a more proactive role in championing the arts of the Highlands and Islands. During that period it will continue to receive the largest allocation of public funding for the arts in the area and it must make sure it uses that to advance the whole of the

Highland arts community. Eden Court has had its adolescence. It has proved to the sceptics it can work – now it must mature, build on its established roots and use its experience to further the cause of others.

Creativity – increasingly recognised as something in which to invest for the benefit of all aspects of society – is Eden Court's core business. We need to work hand in hand with partners in the arts community and the public and private sectors to ensure our work spreads into classrooms and boardrooms. We have plans to improve and develop the building physically over the next five years, to provide the type of facilities and new spaces that will meet the increasingly complex demands of the leisure and cultural market the theatre serves.

The theatre of the 21st century is a difficult building to try and define. As technology increasingly marginalises the communal viewing experience, we have to anticipate and, where possible, lead some of the trends that will ensure Eden Court's relevance.

We have to recognise that the lines which differentiate the arts from other creative and leisure activities are becoming more blurred and, in some cases, inappropriate. The generations who will use the building over the next three decades will look for and expect a different type of experience and service to those in the last quarter-century. Of course, there will always be a place for a core repertoire of live arts experience that is currently impossible to experience in any type of arena other than the theatre as we know it. But that too may change quicker than some of us think – or would like.

August Strindberg, the Swedish dramatist, writing in a preface to "Miss Julie" at the cusp of the 19th and 20th centuries, argued at length for a new type of theatre to be created to cater for the emerging form of naturalism. In his essay he described what we know today as the studio theatre, a more appropriate space for the new observational, emotionally charged theatre he was championing.

One hundred years down the road, the moving image and the broadcasting and electronic media have changed the goalposts radically again. To retain relevance Eden Court has to ensure it keeps a Strindberg-like awareness of the trends of live performance, and cater for them. As it has been in the past 25 years it will involve a great deal of professional and voluntary time, blood, sweat and (always) tears.

There will be argument and disagreement, ups and downs, sweet memories and hasty words – but it will survive and I very much hope to be in the audience at its golden anniversary.

Above
Jim Love, arts editor of the Inverness Courier and author of 'Prize Possession'.

Eden Court in the year 2026...

Jim Love

Inverness Courier.

In case I'm unable to write it - or nobody asks - here's a history of the past 25 years at Eden Court for the theatre's 50th anniversary from the perspective of a theatregoer, who, like any member of an Eden Court audience, evaluates and forms an opinion on the shows they see.

In the first two decades of the 21st century, Inverness experienced a second wave of phenomenal growth matching that of the previous quarter-century and, like the theatre, coverage of Eden Court's activities has increased greatly since 2001. As befits a daily newspaper, the Inverness Courier now carries a daily arts page with a team of journalists providing news, interviews and reviews.

Much of the complex's success can be attributed to the drive of former Eden Court chairman Bryan Beattie who returned to politics in 2011 and is now Scotland's Minister For The Arts and to Colin Marr who, after a decade running the Edinburgh Festival, now crowns a glorious career in arts administration as director of the Barbican Centre in London.

The creation of a new Council headquarters at Beechwood afforded the opportunity in 2019 to build a Music Hall and rehearsal rooms on a site adjacent to the original Eden Court complex which, apart from providing a base for the now fully professional Highland Chamber Orchestra whose concert season complements the activities of the Royal Scottish National Orchestra, the Scottish Chamber Orchestra and the BT Scottish Ensemble, thereby doubling the number of classical concerts held in the Highland Capital and establishing mini-seasons in Dornoch, Wick, Ullpool. Portree Fort William and Kingussie. With a maximum seating capacity of 1500, it is also used for pop concerts, enabling major international acts to perform in the Highland Capital for the first time and serves as an exhibition space, used by conferences or independently for trade and antique fairs, banquets and balls.

Unable to keep pace with the growth in audiences for some of its events, the original Eden Court auditorium - now called The Baxter Theatre - is sufficiently isolated from its Glenurquhart Road extension to enable performances to be held in all three venues simultaneously, the new medium-sized venue, The Beattie Studio, having opened in 2005. It has provided a home and rehearsal space for Theatre Highland, Eden Court's own repertory company, which produces a season of six productions - two classic plays, two contemporary plays and two by Highland writers - as well as offering space to other Highland professional companies like Grey Coast and Tosg and a number of amateur groups including the still-flourishing Florians whose theatre at Bught Park is now used by The Junior Florians.

The Beattie Studio also provides a showcase for local rock bands following in the footsteps of the illustrious Lush Rollers - who, having enjoyed success in the Scottish charts in the first decade of the 21st century, still get together for the occasional reuniuon concert - and to touring jazz musicians who have continued to visit Inverness despite the demise of Inverness Jazz Platform in 2004 and to up-and-coming traditional musicians who have graduated from the thriving session scene in Inverness pubs .

The provision of the medium-sized space having freed up the main auditorium for a greater frequency of major theatrical events, annual visits by the Royal Shakespeare Company and the Scottish National Theatre are eagerly anticipated and well-attended. Inverness-born actor Jimmy Chisholm's "King Lear" was a memorable event. Touring productions of classic whodunnits and West End musicals remain enduringly popular with the older generation who finally saw a professional production of "Cats" in 2019. Lord Mackintosh will stage "The Phantom Of The Opera" later this year for Eden Court's golden jubilee.

The concert celebrating Sir Phil Cunningham's 50 years in show business was another memorable event and the veteran - whose stock of Fergie MacDonald jokes now threatens to reduce his accordion artistry to the level of side-show - is spoken of in the same reverential tones as the legendary Jimmy Shand and is proving an inspiration to a second generation of Féisean students.

Grampian TV continues to make use of the Baxter Theatre for its traditional music series, "The Highland Line". The BBC's satirical comedy series, "Buirbe", is also filmed at Eden Court and the number of independent production companies using its facilities for digital broadcasts has greatly increased. Many of the programmes, including a weekly Highland news bulletin, are sold to stations in the USA, Canada, Australia and New Zealand.

"WHAT EDEN COURT COURT MEANS TO ME"

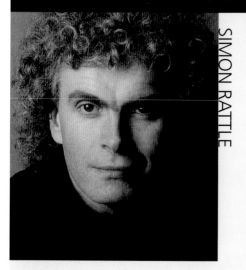

SIMON RATTLE

''The one that got away...''

SIR SIMON RATTLE

Dear Mr Love,

I'm afraid Sir Simon hasn't been able to write something for your book. He has now gone abroad for a couple of weeks. I showed him your e-mail straight away and he was going to try and do something if he had time but unfortunately his rehearsal schedule over the last two weeks was incredibly complicated (together with a lot of other commitments relating to Berlin).

I'm so sorry not to have been able to help.

Best wishes,

Claire Seddon,
PA to Sir Simon Rattle.

The Music Hall's largest of the ancillary studios provides an ideal space for monthly chamber concerts while the hall's other facilities accommodate the music faculty of the University Of The Highlands and Islands and extra-mural learners under the Féisean and Spirit Of Balnain programmes.

The state-of-the-art recording studio has made a major contribution, not just to local creativity but to the local economy, having attracted a succession of international chart-topping acts since it was first used by Madonna for "The Silver Wedding Anniversary Album".

None of these achievements which have placed Inverness firmly on the nation's cultural map would have been possible, however, without continued - and increased - financial support from Highland Council, Highlands & Islands Enterprise and the Scottish Parliament's considerable enlargement of the Scottish Arts Council budget. Also compensating for the diminishing funds available from the National Lottery whose remit has been widened to include social services as well as sport, the arts, health and education, has been a growing number of private sponsors attracted to the area over the past 25 years by the restoration of Inverness's Heathrow airlink and the creation of technology and retail parks at Dalcross, Knocknagael and Dunain Park and by more frequent appearances of the Loch Ness Monster. The theatre's sponsorship officer, appointed in 2000, now has a team of three to maximise this important new source of revenue but it has some way to go yet before matching the levels available to arts organisations in Central Scotland.

Other significant factors in the past quarter-century's developments at Eden Court have been a growth in leisure time, an increasing awareness through education of the value of the arts (triggered in part by Eden Court's expansion in 2005) and an exponential increase in cultural tourism which has led to the Highland Festival's final assumption of the soubriquet "Second only to Edinburgh" - which has, in turn, brought more business to Inverness's Eden Court Centre For The Performing & Traditional Arts and led to the international status it currently enjoys in 2026.

Who would have predicted it when the modest nucleus of the present sprawling but vital complex first opened in 1976 - or, indeed, in 2001 when the theatre celebrated its 25th anniversary?

INDEX

…age numbers in brackets indicate
…n illustration.

5th Anniversary, 106,107
:84 Theatre, 31
:84 Theatre Company, 106
…Love Song for My Lady, 11
…A Theatregoer", 33
…CTivators, 94
…fter School Arts Project, (A.S.A.P.) 94
…lexander, Kenneth, Professor, 47,57
…lexander, Monty, 108
…nderson, Moira, 81
…ntigone', 51
…rchbishop of Canterbury, 58
…rchitects plans and illustrations,
  (19)(20)(21)
…Aristides", 32
…rmstrong, Richard, 107
…rts Centre, 1,10
…rts Theatre, 15
…ssociation of Theatre Unions, 39
…viemore Conference Centre, 31,79,80,88
…BC Big Band, 108
BC Radio Highland, 40
BC Scotland, 57
BC Scottish Symphony Orchestra, 75
…ain, Aly, 73, (72)
…aker, Tom, 91, (92)
…alnain House, 19
…annerman, Charles, 32
…arbirolli, John, 59
…arratt Ayres, Reginald, 37
…arron, Eveline, Miss, 18,22,37,50,51,
  58,59,71,76,84-86,89,111
…atty, John, 95
…auchop, Hamish,Councillor, 50,69,71,
  72,74,76,78,80
…axter, Douglas, Councillor, Rev., 1,9,10,
  12,14 16,18,21,25,27,30,36,45,46,56,
  60,111, (11)
…axter, Margaret, 12,45,60
…ay City Rollers, 51,53
…eattie, Johnny, 55,77
…eattie, Bryan, 102,117
…ell, Jake, 63
…even Baxter, John, 15
…igg, Derek, 13,23,25,26,28,38,39,68,74,
  111, (13)
…rks, Reginald, 45
…shop, Eden, 2, (2)
…ishop's Palace, 2,12,17,19,21,28,49,55,
  85,(8),(12),(49)

Book of Kells, 116
Borderline Theatre Company, 106,
Borge, Victor, 73
Bothy Band, 57
Boxcar Willie, 85
Branagh, Kenneth, 98
Bremner, Andrew, 33
Bridge street, 9,13
Bryden, Bill, 63
Buffer, Bob, 35
Bught Park, 35,53
Building Costs, 25
Building Work In Progress, (34),(41)
Burbage's Theatre, 63
Burstyn, Ellen, 57
Bussell, Darcey, 108,(108)
Byre Theatre St Andrews, 14

Cairns, Norman, 58
Caledonian Associated Cinemas, 5,9
Caledonian Hotel Ballroom, 9,15,55
Cameron, Bud, 27,28,29
Cameron, James, Councillor, 26,35,
  36,39
Cameron of Lochiel, Donald, Sir, 21,39,
  (20)
Campbell, Jack, 10
Campbell MP, Gordon, Lord, 20,27,28,
  (21)
Capercaillie, 108
Carruthers, David, 55,88
Cartoon Forum, 92
Cathedral Players, 10,11, (22)
charitable status, 73,76
Chinese State Circus, 101, (102)
Chisholm, Jimmy, 43,80,82, (82)
Chisholm, Jimmy, Snr., (51)
Church of Scotland, 58
Cinderella, 78
City Lights, 91
Clannad, 108
Clapton, Eric, 15
Clark, Alex, 39,45
Clerk, John, 111
Cliar, 115
Coggan, David, Dr, 58
Common Good Fund, 53,85
Connolly, Billy, 31,73, (72)
Contemporary Dance, 106
Cooper, Gill, 95
Coopers & Lybrand, 85
Corbett, Ronnie, 73, (74)
Corbett, Dan, Councillor, 26,28,48
Countess of Cromarty, 102

County Council Education Dept, 35
Covent Garden, 32,33
Cowan, Robert, Sir, 95
Crator, Dougal, 4, (6)
Crawfords, 71,77
Cream, 15
Crighton Smith, Ian, 91
Crudens Ltd., 35,49,50,68
Cruickshank, Andrew, 55,59,60,73, (52)
Cunningham, Phil, 107, (23),(72)
Current Account, 57
Cuthberson, Iain, 57

Dallas, Donald, 3, (6)
Dancing at Lughnasa, 100, (100)
David, Smith, 95
Davidson, Jim, 108
Death of a Salesman, 10
Dekker, Aileen, Councillor, 73
Dench, Judi, 108
Dickson, Barbara, 73
District Council Chief Executive,69
Dodd, Ken, 108
Don, Scott, 4,84
Don Giovanni, 55,107, (106)
Donald, Peter, 12,31,46,71,83,84,86, (84)
Doonican, Val, 85, (85)
Doyle, John, 15,55,77,77, (55)
Doyle, Molly, 102
D'Oyly Carte, 39,40,73,75,84
Dr Finlay's Casebook, 55, (52)
Drama Artist in Residence, 95
Drummond, Peter, 27,36,53,74
Dubliners, The, 108
Duke and Duchess of York, 113
Dunbar, Sandy, 18,78,83
Dunbar-Nasmith, David, 20
Dunbar-Nasmith, James, Sir, 18-20,35,59,
  86,101,111,113, (26)
Duncan, Sandy, 21
Dundee Repertory Theatre, 106

Earl of Cromartie, 23
East, Donald, 58
Easterbrook, A J, 39
Easton, Sheena, 87-88
Eden Court Appeal Fund, 25,26,35
Eden Court Board of Governors,
  45,56,60,71,72,74,76,78-81,84 86,
  88,89,95,102
Eden Court Opening Gala, 57-59, (1)
Eden Court Theatre, (121)
Edgar Broughton Band, 57
Edinburgh International Festival, 37
Edinburgh Opera House, 26,37
Edmond, Stuart, 39

Edwards, Jimmy, 84
Edwards, Murray, 45,47,51,53,64,71,73,
  74,76-79,94,107,(45),(112)
Elton, Ben, 108
Empire Theatre, 2,3,9,10-11,15,17,31,56,
  (3),(16)
Episcopal Bishop, of Moray Ross &
  Caithness, 2
Equity, 45
European Community Public Fund, 53
European Economic Community, (EEC),
  50
European Regional Development Fund,
  (ERDF), 53
Exorcist, The, 40

Falcon, Val, 76,78,88,100, (77)
Fascinating Aida, 100
Fasken, Robert (Bobby), 21,47,80,81,95,
  (46)
Fiddes QC, J R, 38,40
Finance Committee, 37,54,56,72
firm contract, 57,65
Five Guys Named Moe, 69,98,102, (90)
fixed contract, 57,65
Flemming, Tom, 108
Flood, Gerald, 57
Flora MacDonald YMCA Hall, 7
Florians,The, 9,10,15,40,57,74 (23),(33)
fly tower, 59,88
Forrest, Robert, 21
Fraser, Jack, Councillor, 9
Fraser, Margaret, Councillor, 27
Fraser, Ian, Provost and Councillor, 27,36,
  37,46,48,53,56,60,79,83,111, (36)
Fraser, William, Provost and Treasurer,
  25-28,32,33,37,40,45,50,53,68,82
  86,101,111,113, (26)
Free Presbyterian Church, 1
Friedman, Leonard, 72
Friends of Eden Court, 2,3,47,48,56,73,
  83,85,87,94,98
Fuchs, Lisa, 95
Fulton, Rikki, 16,77
Fyfe, Will, 3

Gallway, James, 2,35,73,82,97, (3)
Gardiner, Derek, 35,49,50, (48)
Gayle, Chrystall, 108
General Election, 40
Gibson, Alexander, 60
Gilchrist, Andrew, Sir, 31,47
Gilchrist, Lady, 31
Gillespie, Kieran, 95

Gillies, Alasdair, 16,81, (16)
Gillies, Anne Lorne, (55)
Glass, Jack, Pastor, 73
Glennie, Evelyn, 97
Goldman, William, 92, (93)
Gould, Clio, 61, (61)
Gowans, Flora, 31,32
Grampian TV, 63
Grappelli, Stephan, 73,79,83
Gray, Andy, 91, (93)
'Green Lady, The', 65
Grieve, John, 63
Guiness, Alec, 2
Gulbenkian Foundation, 12

'Hair', 63,71,77
Hamilton, Alastair, 63
Hamilton, George, 87, (88)
Hamilton, Lindsay, 10,31,39
Hamilton, Scott, 108
Hampshire, Susan, 108
Hay, Patricia, 60,89, (89)
Hedda Gabler, 98
Henry, Lenny, 108
Highland and Island Development
  Board,(HIDB),12,15,17,20,21,38,39,40,
  47,48,51,57,77,82,95
Highland Council, 105
Highland County Council, 2,2,17
Highland District Council, 1,53,56,57
Highland Festival, (114)
Highland Health Board, 74
Highland News, The, 56,95
Highland Regional Council, 1,2,46,47,53,
  54,56,57
Highland sports club, 10
Hill, Isla, 35,36
Hill, John R, Town Clerk, 15,21,25,26,27,
  35,(35)
Hill, Vince, 73
Hillman, David, 60
Historic Inverness, 31
HM The Queen, 113
HM The Queen Mother, 25,35
Hooker, Craigmyle & Co, 19
Hospital Board, 17
"house of vanity", 28,29,31,39
HRH Duchess of Kent, 77
HRH Prince Philip, 113
HRH Princess Alexandra, 73
HRH Princess Anne, 113
Hume, Alan, Sir, 38
Hunter, Bill, 31
Hunter, Mollie, 10,11,15, (11)

Hunter, Russell, 1,16,28,45,60, (60)
Hunter, James, Dr, 115, (115)

I.R.S.F., (110)
"Icarus", 29,31
Imlah, Alan, 51,86
Inflation, 1,28
Inverness Amenities Association, 19
Inverness Arts Guild, 15,40
Inverness Caledonian Footballer, 9,16
Inverness Choral Society, 31,43,84
Inverness County Council, 39
Inverness Courier, 9-10,1418,25-32,37,47
51,53-55, 58,59,71-74,77,85-89,
102,105
Inverness District Council, 37,46-48,
50,72,78,85
Inverness Film Club, 46
Inverness Folk Festival, 57
Inverness High School, 57
Inverness Jazz Platform, 64,74,107
Inverness Motor Company, 31
Inverness Music Festival, 57
Inverness Music Society, 15,21,31,35,58
Inverness Opera Company, 9,15,21,45,
55,74,84, (10),(43)
Inverness Royal Academy, 15,43,55
Inverness Strathspey and Reel Society, 46
Inverness Town Council, 2,7,9-12,15,
17,19,21,22,25,27 33,38,45,51,53,
68,107
Irons, Forbes, 5
Izzard, Eddie, 108, (108)

Jack, William, 14,39
Jacobi, Derek, 60, (57)
Jaffery, James, 48,49
Jeff Beck Group, 15
John, Alan, 88
Johnson, Chris, 79-82,84,88,91,107,
(80)
Johnston, Russell, MP, 16,56,57,65,68,
(56)
Jones, Paul, 65, (68)
Jones, Jack, 82

Keane, Dillie, 100
Keith, Francis, Councillor, 54
Kelly, Janis, 15,42,74,(42),
Kelly, Louise, 77 (77)
Kelly, Peter, 43
Kennedy, Calum, 9,55
Kennedy, Fiona, 55
Kennedy, Nigel, 97, (98)
Kennedy, Mary Anne, (114)
Kidd, Carol, 108
King, Bob, 26
Kirk, Rhona, 94, (80)

La Scala, 9,16,40,58
La Travatia, 10
Lang, Matheson, 3,59, (3)
'Lasair Dhe', 115
Lauder, Harry, Sir, 3
Law, Graham, 18-20,21,35,49,101
Law, Phyllida, 98, (99)
Law and Dunbar Nasmith, 18,101, (19)
Lazarev, Alexander, 95, (96)
Lesiure and Recreation Committee, 46,47,
50,53
Little Theatre, The,1,15,29,31,35,45,46,
55, 58
Lloyd, Freddie, 84
Lloyd Webber, Julian, 97
Local Government (Scotland) Act, 1973,
68
Logan, Jimmy, 64,65,73,79,80-82,91,
(Foreward),(62)

Long Gallery, 85
Love, Jim, 119, (118)
Lyon, Ron, Councillor, 27,30,48,64, (26)
Lyttleton, Humphrey, 79, 113, (113)

MacArthur, Helen, 57
MacAskil, Iain, 47
MacCallum, David, 108
MacCallum, Kenneth, 86
MacDonald, Andrew J., "Resident",
32,33,38,39,40,46,111, (38)
MacDonald, Norman Malcolm, 91
Macdonald, Dr, 25
MacDonald, Calum, (50)
MacInnes, Janet, 101
Mackay, Bert, 88, (88)
Mackay, William, 28,31,
Mackay, William, Councillor and Provost,
9,56,75,111,(9)
MacKenzie, Compton, 91
Mackenzie, Tom, 26,28, (26)
Mackenzie, David and Kristine, 77,81,88
Mackintosh, Cameron, Sir, 69,98,102,
(69)
Mackintosh of Mackintosh, Councillor,
81,(83)
MacLean, Colin, 37
MacLean, Una, 80
MacLeary, Donald, 57,60,79,83,(58)
Macleod, Kenneth, Councillor, 16,26
MacMillan, Roddy, 63
MacNeacail, Aonghas, 91
MacPhee, Richie, 27
MacQueen, Eona, 111
MacQueen, Ewan A., 28-33,37-40
46,53,111, (37)
Mactaggart, Archie, 105
Manse Place, 10
Marc Bolan , (14)
Mardon Roland, Councillor, 71,81
Margaret Firth School of Dancing, 45,57
Marketing Review, (86)
Marks & Spencers, 83
Marr, Colin, 103,105-107, (104),(112)
Marshall, Arthur, 48
Martin, J H, 25
Matheson, Donald, 4
Maurel, Paul, 100,102,103,107, (101)
Mayall, Rik, 108
McCue, Bill, 60
McElhone, Frank, 57,65
McKay, W J, Provost, 9,10,12,15, (9)
McKuen, Rod, 75,76
Melly, George, 83
Menuhin, Yehudi, 55,82,(83)
Mermaid Theatre, 10
Merton, Paul, 108
MIDB, 31
Miller, James, 94, (95)
Miller, Ian, Chief Executive and Councillor,
47,51,64, (52)
Miller, Hugh, 37
Milne, Alastair, Councillor, 12,26,31,35,
55,71, (12),(31)
Milroy, Jack, 74
Mouskouri, Nana, 108
Mitford Trophy, 11
Monkhouse, Bob, 95, (95)
Moray Firth, 12
Morrison, Peter, 53,77
Morrison (QC) A. M., 38,39,40
Moscow City Ballet, (70)
Moss, Eric, Councillor, Major, 54
Move, The, 15
Movie Makers, 92
Mrs Brown, 92

Mulroy, Jack, 16
Munro, Caroline, 92
Munro, Louise, (33)
Murray, Chic, (73)
Murray, David, Councillor, 36
Music Hall, The, 2

Nairn District Council, 32,48
Nairn Tourist Association, 48
Nairnshire Telegraph, 48
National Mod, The, 31
National Theatre, 39,63,92
Ness River Rhythm Kings, 74
Niall, Duncan MacKillop 'Icarus', 31
Nicholson, Murdo, Reverend, 46
Nicoll, Harry, 15, (15)
Nicolson, Murdo, Councillor, Rev.,1,54,
113, (55)
Niven, Roger, 95
Nordring Music Prize, 57
Northern Hospitals Board of
Management, 46
Northern Meeting Rooms, 9
Northern Meeting Society, 2,47,64
Nottingham Civic Theatre, 39

O'Donnell, Daniel, 105, 108
Oh! Calcutta!, 85
Ohara, Noriko, 43, (43)
Oil Boom, 2
Opera for all, 10
Out of Eden, 94
Outreach, 94
Oxford Playhouse, 57

Pantomime, 65,73,76,81,83
Para Handy, 91
Parfit, Gerald, 27,31
Patsy Cline, 53
Pena, Paco, 73
Perlemuter, Vlado, 15
Petchey, John, 95,100, (103)
'Peter & The Wolf', 1, (1)
Phase II Studio Theatre, 50
Phillips, Sian, 108
Phoenix Drama Club, 17,46, (51)
Pitlochry Festival Theatre, 78
Planning & Development Committee,
9,13,14
Playhouse, The, 9,17,19
Playhouse Cinema, 3
Policy and Resources Committee, 53,54,
64,73,79
Pollitt, Gerald, Councillor, 12
Polwarth, Lord, 35
Porteous, John, 40
Press and Journal, 95
Pride, Charley, 108
Pringle, James, 9,74, (10)
"prize possession", 54, 113
Proclaimers, The, 108
programmes, (66-67)
Project, Theatre Company, 1
Provost Smith Trust, 79,
Provost's Benevolent Fund, 73
Public Relations Officer, 2,55

Queens Park, 10
Quinn, Nick, 76

Raigmore Hospital, 31,32
"Ratepayer", 28
Rattle, Simon, 75,120, (78),(120)
Redmond, Moira, 60
Rendle, Adrian, 63
"Resident", 29,30,32
restaurant, 11,77,88,102
Rhind, Isobel, Councillor, 54, (54)
Rhythms of the North, 94

Richmond, Fiona, 84
Richter, Sviatoslav, 73,75, (75)
Riddell, Donald, 46
Rising Inflation, 40
River Ness, 2
Riverside Screen, 94
Rob Roy, 3
Robbins, Catherine, 91,98,107, (92)
Robertson, Edwin, (47)
Robertson, John, Councillor, 48,54
Robertson, Toby, 1
Robson, Flora, Dame, 80
Rod Stewart, 15, (14)
Rodgers, Annie, 19
Rogart Amateur Dramatic Society, 58
Rose, Sonia, 94, (94)
Ross, Annie, 73
Ross, Ann Louise, 80
Ross, William, 17,35
Ross, Lachlan, 76
Ross & Cromarty, 2
Rotary Club, 35
Royal Ballet, 57, 108
Royal Gala, 73
Royal Lyceum Theatre, 57,63
Royal Scottish National Orchestra, 95
Royal Shakespeare Company, 14
Royal Shakespeare Company, 91,92
Runrig, 50,85,108,(87)

Sadlers Wells, 14,32
safety curtain, 59,100
Saville, Jimmy, OBE, 31, (30)
'"Savoyard", 32
Scobie, Gavin, 76
Scotsman, The, 63
Scott, Colin, 101
Scott Robinson, Stanley, Sheriff, 85,
Scottish Arts Council, 2,3,13-17,18,39,
40,44-51,64,71,72,76,77, 81-85,91,
94,105,106
Scottish Ballet, 57,71,76,79,84,91,106
Scottish Baroque Ensemble, 72
Scottish Brewers, 83
Scottish Chamber Orchestra, 57,64,73,
77,97
Scottish Community Drama Association,
SCDA, 10,31,39,57,63
Scottish Development Department, 21
Scottish Ensemble, 61
Scottish Film Council, 47,51
Scottish National Orchestra, 3,7,10,15,
47,51,60,63,71,73,83
Scottish Office, 17,26,48,51,53,64
Scottish Opera, 55,57,58,78,71,
91,106,107
Scottish Secretary, 25-28,31,32,35-40,
65,68
Scottish Tourist Board, 25
sculpture, 76
Secombe, Harry, 83
Secretary State for Scotland, 1,17,20
Sellar, Allan, Provost and Councillor, 27,
50,68,76,83,86,88,111
Shaw Grant, James, 82,100,101, (82)
Sievwright, Brian, 82
Silver, George, 95, (98)
Skinner, Mabel, Councillor, 27,72,77,
(27)
Sleep, Wayne, 91
Smith, William, Provost and Councillor,
1,26, 35,36,39,12,25,27,29, 31,33,
45,47,48,56,60,68,111,115 (13),(24)
Smith, John, MP, (111)
Smith, Tom, Councillor, 12
Smith, Carola, 59

"Smiths Folly", 1,29,32
Social Work Committee, 54
Souter, Graham, 31
Souter & Jaffrey, 18,35
South China Post, 63
"Sportswoman", 29
Starféis, 94 (94)
Steel Shortages, 49
Stevens, Cat, 15
Stevenson, Ronald, 69(79)
STUC, 39,40
Studio theatre, 106
Sunday Times, The, 63
Swanson, William, Councillor, 46
Syd Lawrence Orchestra, 73
Sykes, Eric, 84

The Alexander Brothers, 74, (75)
The Byre, St Andrews, 92
The Entertainer, 92
'The Gondoliers', 43
The New Seekers, 73
The Playhouse, 28
Theatre refurbishment, 101
Theatre Royal, 2,3,28
Thompson, Emma, 98, (99)
Thomson, Kennedy, 63
Three day week, 1,40,49
Thurso Players, 58
Tie Up Theatre Company, 55,58,77
Tocher, Gordon, 43
Todd, Richard, 108
Tomsett, Simon, 95
'Top of the Form', 32
Tortelier, Paul, 84
Town Council, 35-40,43
Town House, 13,15,17,25,33,53
'Trainspotting', 92

Urquhart, Robert, 39
Urquhart, Jean, 101
Urquhart, Margaret, 31

Vaughan, Frankie, 84
Venegerov, Maxim, 97, (97)

Walker, Kenneth, Councillor, 21
Watson, Jonathan, 91, (93)
Webb, Marti, 91
Weir, James, 10
Weller, Walter, 97
Wells, Doreen, 57,60
West, Timothy, 60, (61)
What's On guides, (67)
"white elephant", 28,32,51,113
Willams, Don, 108
Wilmot, Gary, 108
Wilson, Brian, 85
Wilson, Robert, (7)
Wilton, Penelope, 60
Wolfstone, 108,(109)
Wordsworth, William, 56
Work In Progress, (44)(46)
Worth, John, 5,11,81,84, (7),(11),
Wraight, Tony, 74
Wright, Allen, 63
Wyckham, John, 1,10,14,15,18,27,35,
39,49,50,60,71,78,106, (14)
Wynette, Tammy, 108

X-Factor Dance Company, (105)

Young, Margaret, 21,31
Yvonne Arnaud Theatre, 10

Contents

Chapter 1   Universal genius   4

Chapter 2   From student to doctor   12

Chapter 3   Cosmology and the universe   18

Chapter 4   Discoveries and prizes   24

Chapter 5   Trials and triumphs   30

Chapter 6   A theory of everything   38

Glossary   46

Find out more   47

Index   48

Chapter 1

universal genius

Stephen Hawking's life, work and ideas make for a remarkable story. He is widely regarded as one of the world's most brilliant theoretical physicists. His work on the origins and structure of the universe, from the big bang to black holes, has revolutionized our understanding of the workings of space and time. He has taken huge steps towards unifying the two greatest theories of physics – Albert Einstein's theory of general relativity, which governs the large-scale universe, and quantum mechanics, which governs the universe of the unimaginably small.

Hawking has achieved all this while suffering from a condition that has left him incapable of movement or speech. At the age of 21, he was diagnosed with amyotrophic lateral sclerosis (ALS), a form of motor neuron disease. The secrets of the universe unfold in Hawking's head, communicated to the world through a computer and speech synthesizer activated by tiny twitches of a cheek muscle.

Wow!

Stephen Hawking has become one of the most recognized scientists in the world today.

Celebrity scientist

Hawking once said, "My goal is simple. It is a complete understanding of the universe, why it is as it is and why it exists at all." He has probably come as close as any scientist to achieving this understanding. In the process, he has become perhaps the best-known scientist since Albert Einstein and has made science much more popular, talked about and understood.

STAR CONTRIBUTION

Now in his 70s, Hawking still carries out his research into theoretical physics and travels the world to give lectures on his findings. He also has great ambitions to make it into space one day and perhaps also to have his brain encoded onto a computer. Speaking at the premiere of a documentary about his life in 2013, he said, "I think the brain is like a program in the mind, which is like a computer, so it's theoretically possible to copy the brain onto a computer and so provide a form of life after death."

Born in wartime

Stephen William Hawking was born on 8 January 1942. This was the 300th anniversary of the death of the great Italian scientist Galileo, who first used a telescope to observe the moons of Jupiter and the craters of the Moon. Hawking is quite proud of this shared anniversary.

Hawking's parents lived in Highgate, in north London. When Hawking was due to be born, it was the middle of World War II, and the German airforce was carrying out regular bombing raids on London. Hawking's father, Frank, decided London was far too hazardous a place to be when his wife gave birth and moved his family to the relative safety of Oxford. It was there that Stephen Hawking was born.

Hawking was born 300 years to the day after the death of Galileo, one of the fathers of modern physics.

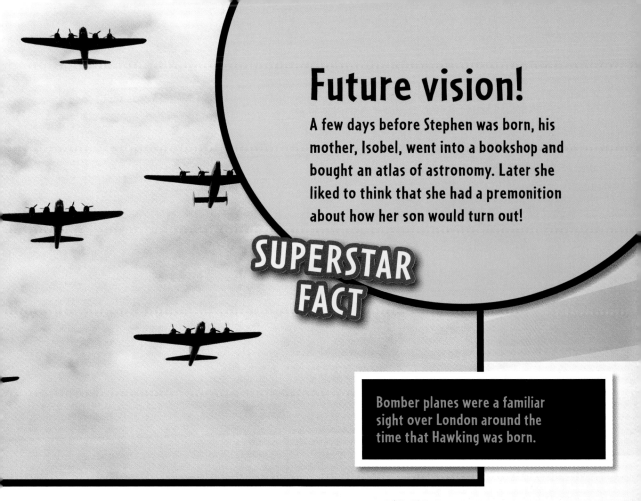

Future vision!

A few days before Stephen was born, his mother, Isobel, went into a bookshop and bought an atlas of astronomy. Later she liked to think that she had a premonition about how her son would turn out!

SUPERSTAR FACT

Bomber planes were a familiar sight over London around the time that Hawking was born.

Isobel Hawking, Stephen's mother, had graduated from the University of Oxford, where she studied economics, philosophy and politics. Oxford had only been granting degrees to women since 1920, and the 1930s, when Isobel was a student, were a time when few women went to university. Stephen's father, who had studied medical science, was also an Oxford graduate. Neither of their families were wealthy and both had struggled to find the money to send their children to university.

Hawking's parents met at a medical institute in London, where Isobel was a medical secretary and Frank was a respected medical researcher, specializing in tropical diseases. They were married just after the war started. Hawking's first sister, Mary, was born 18 months after he was, and his other sister, Philippa, was born when he was nearly 5. Hawking describes her as a "very perceptive child" and says that he has always respected her judgement and opinions. Hawking also has a brother, Edward, who was adopted by the family when Hawking was 14.

First school days

The Hawkings returned to Highgate, in London, soon after Stephen was born. The war was still going on and London could be dangerous. On one occasion, just after the birth of Mary Hawking, the family had a lucky escape when a German rocket exploded near their home. Sharp shards of glass blew in from the back windows and embedded in the wall opposite. Fortunately, only Frank Hawking was in the house and he was unhurt.

Crash!

The German bombing of London hit all parts of the city, including Highgate, where the Hawkings lived.

The war had ended by the time Hawking started going to school, at the age of four. He attended Byron House School in Highgate, which he describes as "very progressive" for the time. Most of the other children there also had parents who were scientists or academics. Hawking recalls complaining to his parents that he was not learning anything at Byron House – "You were supposed to learn to read without realizing you were being taught." In the end, he did not learn to read until the age of eight. His sister Philippa could read when she was four, but, as Hawking says, "She was definitely brighter than me."

Hawking has said that he and his sister Mary were always rivals, probably because they were so close in age. The competition between them only lessened in adulthood, when they followed very different career paths – Stephen into theoretical physics and his sister into medicine as a doctor.

Knowing the ins and outs

Soon after moving into the new house in St. Albans, Stephen had worked out 11 possible ways to get in and out of his home. His sister Mary only ever worked out ten of them.

SUPERSTAR STAT

Frank Hawking's career meant that he was often away from home for months at a time as he took regular trips to Africa to carry out his research into tropical diseases. Stephen's sister Mary thought their father was like a bird that migrates in winter, returning home when the weather turned warmer! In 1950, Frank, after 11 years at the National Institute for Medical Research, became a department head when the important scientific research body moved to Mill Hill, on the northern edge of London. The family, in turn, made the move to St. Albans, a small city about 30 kilometres (20 miles) north of Highgate.

Little Einstein

Hawking was eight when his family arrived in St. Albans. It is one of England's oldest cities, with a cathedral that dates back more than 1,700 years and even older foundations, built on the site of the Roman city of Verulamium.

The house the Hawkings moved into was big and rambling. For a family home, however, it had few luxuries and was always in need of repair. There was no proper heating – if people were cold, Frank Hawking simply insisted that they put on extra layers of clothes. One thing the Hawkings' home definitely had, however, was plenty of books. Visitors to the house reported that the family members usually had their head in a book, even when having their meals at the dining table.

Hawking's classmates had no idea how much influence the ideas of Albert Einstein would have on him in later life.

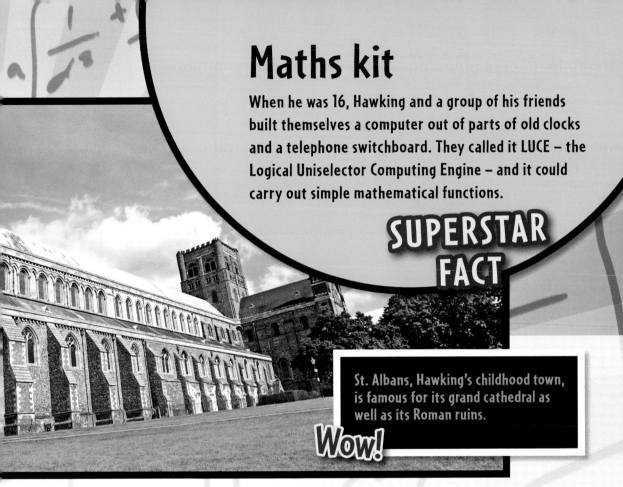

Maths kit

When he was 16, Hawking and a group of his friends built themselves a computer out of parts of old clocks and a telephone switchboard. They called it LUCE – the Logical Uniselector Computing Engine – and it could carry out simple mathematical functions.

SUPERSTAR FACT

St. Albans, Hawking's childhood town, is famous for its grand cathedral as well as its Roman ruins.

Wow!

Hawking attended St. Albans High School for Girls (which took boys up to the age of ten) and then moved to St. Albans School. His untidy work and poor handwriting gave his teachers headaches but, as if they knew what was to come, Hawking's classmates nicknamed him "Einstein".

When Hawking was 13, his father wanted him to try for a place at the prestigious Westminster School in London. As his parents were not wealthy, he needed to win a scholarship in order to attend. Hawking was ill at the time of the scholarship examination, however, and did not take it. He later said that the education he got at St. Albans was just as good as he could have expected at Westminster.

When it came time to choose a university course, Hawking wanted to specialize in mathematics and physics. His father, however, was against this. The final decision to study physics and chemistry with "just a little mathematics thrown in" would eventually lead to Hawking having to develop the maths skills he needed for his later research virtually on his own.

Chapter 2

From student to doctor

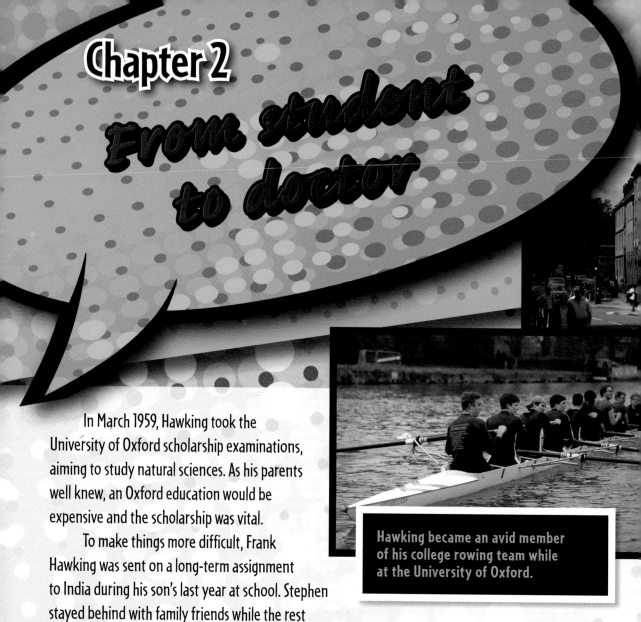

Hawking became an avid member of his college rowing team while at the University of Oxford.

In March 1959, Hawking took the University of Oxford scholarship examinations, aiming to study natural sciences. As his parents well knew, an Oxford education would be expensive and the scholarship was vital.

To make things more difficult, Frank Hawking was sent on a long-term assignment to India during his son's last year at school. Stephen stayed behind with family friends while the rest of the Hawkings went abroad. The head teacher at St. Albans thought that Stephen should wait another year before taking the scholarship exams, but he decided to go ahead with them. A few days after completing the exams, Hawking received a telegram – he had the scholarship.

In October 1959, at the age of 17, Hawking took up his place at University College, Oxford, where he specialized in physics in his natural sciences degree. He described the University of Oxford as being very "anti-work" – if you were naturally brilliant enough you would get a good degree, but actually working hard for one was frowned upon.

Easy does it

Hawking calculated that over the three years he spent studying at Oxford he did about 1,000 hours of work – an average of an hour a day.

SUPERSTAR STAT

The University of Oxford is recognized as being one of the top five universities in the world.

In his second year, Hawking took up rowing. He did not have the physical strength to row but he could be the cox of the rowing team, steering and shouting out orders to the boat's eight rowers. Rowing gave Hawking a real sense of belonging and he became happier and more relaxed.

As the end of his time at Oxford approached, Hawking had been accepted for a place at Cambridge to study for his doctorate – but only if he secured a first class degree from Oxford. With the final exams looming, he started to study harder than ever before. When the results came in, Hawking was on the border between a first-class and a second-class degree. The examiners called him to an interview. Feeling confident, Hawking declared, "If I get a First, I shall go to Cambridge. If I receive a Second, I will remain at Oxford. So I expect that you will give me a First." He got his first class degree!

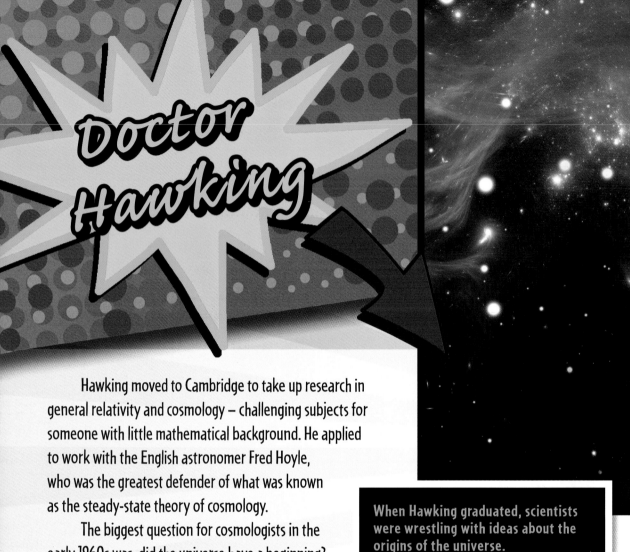

Doctor Hawking

Hawking moved to Cambridge to take up research in general relativity and cosmology – challenging subjects for someone with little mathematical background. He applied to work with the English astronomer Fred Hoyle, who was the greatest defender of what was known as the steady-state theory of cosmology.

The biggest question for cosmologists in the early 1960s was, did the universe have a beginning? Many scientists were opposed to the idea. They could not see how science could describe the event that created the universe. That was something that belonged to religion.

It turned out that Hoyle could not take on any more students, so Hawking had to study under English physicist Dennis Sciama. Hawking had not heard of Sciama, but he would prove to be a strong supporter and Hawking came to enjoy the friendly and supportive environment Sciama created for his students.

Because Hawking had not done much maths at school, and there had been little in his physics course at Oxford, Sciama suggested that he work on astrophysics. But Hawking had come

Blazing a trail

When deciding between studying particle physics, which looks at the behaviour of subatomic particles, or cosmology – not a popular subject at the time – Hawking chose cosmology because, he said, particle physics "seemed like botany. There were all these particles, but no theory."

In 1963, it seemed as if ALS might bring Hawking's career, and life, to an early end.

to Cambridge to study cosmology, and that was what he was going to do. He read old textbooks and travelled every week to lectures at King's College, London.

During his last year at Oxford, Hawking noticed that he was getting clumsy and sometimes had difficulty talking. When he went home for Christmas in 1962, his family saw something was wrong and persuaded him to see a doctor. Early in 1963, Hawking was diagnosed as having ALS, a condition that affects nerve cells in the brain and spinal cord, leading to gradual loss of all muscle control. The doctors predicted that Hawking would not live more than a few years.

Love and ambition

During Hawking's first two years at Cambridge, his condition grew worse. He found it hard to get around and had to use a stick to help him walk. Dennis Sciama remembered how Hawking would often turn up to college with his head bandaged after a fall. His speech was affected, too, and even close friends struggled to understand what he was saying.

Around the same time he was diagnosed with ALS, Hawking met a woman called Jane Wilde at a New Year's Eve party in St. Albans. A few days later he invited her to his 21st birthday party. The two were soon seeing much more of each other and got engaged in October 1964. This was a turning point in Hawking's life. He realized that if he was going to get married, he would have to get a job, and that meant finishing his PhD, or doctorate. According to Hawking, "I started working for the first time in my life."

SUPERSTAR FACT

Tripping up teacher

Hawking's ALS certainly did not affect his mind. On one occasion, in 1964, Hawking turned up at a meeting where Fred Hoyle was giving a talk on his latest ideas on the steady-state theory. In front of everyone, Hawking pointed out flaws in Hoyle's mathematics. Hoyle was not pleased – but Hawking turned out to be right.

Wow!

In the mid 1960s, Hawking began to study the mysterious regions of space called black holes.

At one point, Hawking's father, Frank, visited Dennis Sciama and asked if there was any way Stephen could complete his doctorate in fewer than three years. Sciama said this was impossible. He had seen what a big difference Jane Wilde had made to Hawking's outlook on life, however, and Sciama really believed that he would find the determination to achieve his goal.

Another boost to Hawking's work was his meeting with English physicist Roger Penrose. Penrose had been applying his mathematical skills to studying what happened when a massive object, such as a star, collapses under its own gravity. Hawking was also working on some ideas about these mysterious objects. As it happened, Penrose's brother was a friend of Dennis Sciama, and Penrose and Hawking were introduced. They would form a partnership to study what became known as "black holes".

Chapter 3

Cosmology and the universe

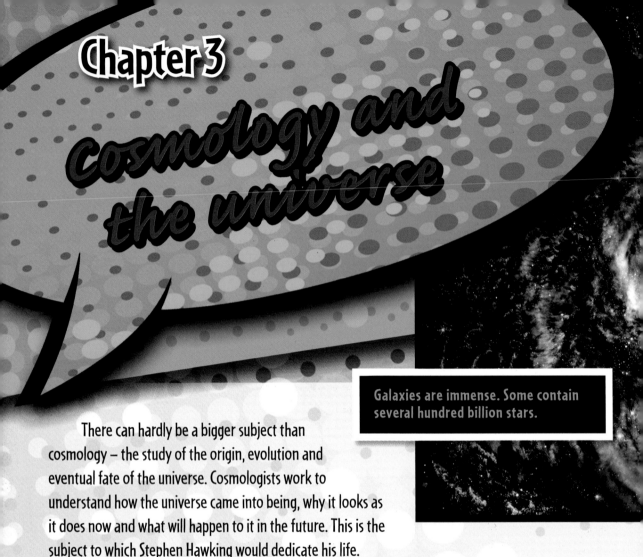

Galaxies are immense. Some contain several hundred billion stars.

There can hardly be a bigger subject than cosmology – the study of the origin, evolution and eventual fate of the universe. Cosmologists work to understand how the universe came into being, why it looks as it does now and what will happen to it in the future. This is the subject to which Stephen Hawking would dedicate his life.

Cosmologists are not concerned with single stars and planets, or even galaxies. They want to know the answers to the big questions. How big is the universe? Where did it come from? Will it last forever? Is all we can see all that there is?

Our ideas about the structure of the universe changed in the 1920s, when astronomers such as the Edwin Hubble began exploring space with powerful new telescopes. Hubble found that stars are not distributed evenly through space, but are gathered together in huge clusters called galaxies. By measuring the light from these galaxies, Hubble could work out how fast they were moving. He expected that they would be moving randomly, with as many moving towards us as are moving away. To his surprise, Hubble found that not only were the galaxies moving away from us, but also the further away they were the faster they were moving. The universe was expanding.

Big bang beginnings

Scientists have estimated that the big bang happened around 14 billion years ago. It took around another 400 million years for the first stars to form.

SUPERSTAR STAT

EDWIN HUBBLE
ASTRONOMER

sa 41

The US astronomer Edwin Hubble was the first person to discover that the universe is expanding.

When Stephen Hawking went to Cambridge there were two conflicting ideas about the origins of the universe. One, called the steady-state theory, said that the universe expanded, but as it did so new matter was being created all the time, so the amount of matter in any particular region of space stayed more or less the same over time.

The other idea, called the big bang theory, said that the universe had begun as a tiny point of energy and had been expanding outwards ever since. As no new matter was created, the galaxies were gradually moving apart from each other and space was becoming emptier. All the evidence we have today points towards the big bang theory being the correct one.

Black holes revealed

In 1966, Hawking earned his PhD in physics. He did so by completing a piece of work called a dissertation, which was entitled "Occurrence of Singularities in Cosmology." The dissertation built on Roger Penrose's work on black holes.

A black hole is a place in space where the force of gravity is so powerful that not even light can escape from it. The name "black hole" is usually credited to US physicist John Wheeler, who coined the term in a 1967 lecture.

Whoosh!

Black holes are invisible – but we may be able to detect them from the matter that falls into them.

Black holes form when a big star comes to the end of its life. The outer part of the star explodes out into space as a supernova, leaving the dense core (centre) of the star behind. When the star was active, the nuclear energy it produced was enough to keep the force of gravity from causing the star to collapse in on itself. Without that energy, the core of the star begins to collapse into a smaller and smaller space, becoming more and more dense until it forms a "singularity". This is a point in space that is infinitely small and infinitely dense. All of the matter that made up the core of the star is packed into a tiny point even smaller than an atom.

Big bang proof

Hawking and Penrose showed that if the description of the universe given by Albert Einstein's theory of general relativity was correct, then the universe must have begun with a singularity. The two physicists came up with mathematical proof that the universe had indeed begun with a "big bang" as the singularity exploded outwards.

STAR CONTRIBUTION

The boundary marking the limits of a black hole is called the "event horizon". This is the distance from the singularity at which its gravitational pull is so strong that light itself is trapped by it. Since nothing can escape from within the event horizon, we cannot know what is happening inside it.

After completing his doctorate in 1966, Hawking was awarded a fellowship in theoretical physics at Gonville and Caius College, Cambridge. He and Penrose worked together on their joint ideas about singularities and the origins of the universe. Penrose had developed new mathematical techniques to explain how space and time are curved by a singularity. Hawking then took these ideas and applied them to the whole universe.

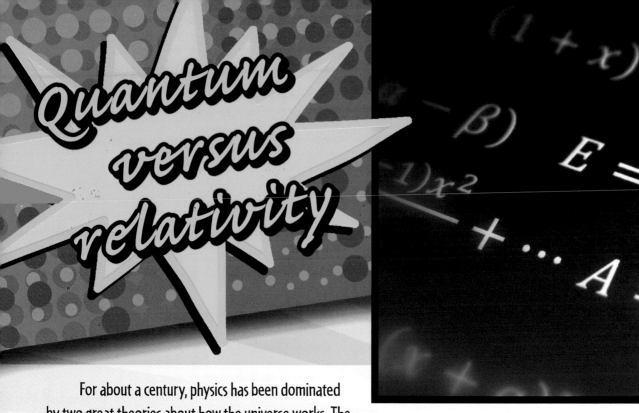

Quantum versus relativity

For about a century, physics has been dominated by two great theories about how the universe works. The first of these, Einstein's theory of general relativity, looks at things on a grand scale, describing how gravity shapes the universe of space and time. The second, quantum mechanics, describes how the universe works on the very smallest scale, down to the size of atoms and even smaller.

Both theories work extremely well. They have been tested by observation and experiment to extraordinary levels of accuracy and each one of them seems to reflect the universe as it actually is. The problem facing physicists is that the two theories just do not join up. The laws of relativity that govern the universe on the large scale do not apply on the small scale of quantum mechanics. The opposite is also true – quantum mechanics tells us nothing about the movements of galaxies. At the moment, there is no theory that successfully combines gravity with quantum mechanics.

All the matter and energy in the universe were created by the big bang, 14.6 billion years ago.

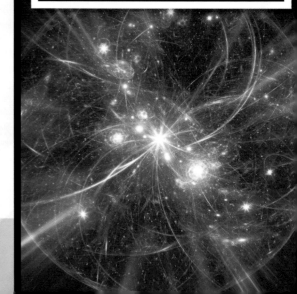

Super small

When considering conditions in the early universe, Hawking was thinking on an incredibly small scale. At its very start, the universe was just a billion trillion trillionth of a centimetre across.

SUPERSTAR STAT

Wow!

Einstein's theories help us to understand how the universe works on a grand scale.

It was Hawking's ambition to find a way to unite the two theories, especially through his studies of black holes and singularities. His and Penrose's results showed that Einstein's theory of general relativity predicted that the universe started as a singularity. They also showed, however, that relativity does not apply in the immensely strong gravitational fields that were present in the early, very small and dense universe. At this scale, quantum mechanics has to be taken into account.

Hawking developed the idea that the quantum creation of the universe could be imagined as being like bubbles of steam in boiling water, appearing and then disappearing. Some universes were like these bubbles, only expanding so far and then collapsing and vanishing again. These alternative universes would not last long enough for stars or galaxies to appear, and certainly not long enough for the development of intelligent life. Some bubbles, however, would grow big enough to avoid collapsing. They would go on expanding at an ever-increasing rate, with tiny irregularities in the bubble leading to the formation of planets, stars, galaxies and life.

Chapter 4

Discoveries and prizes

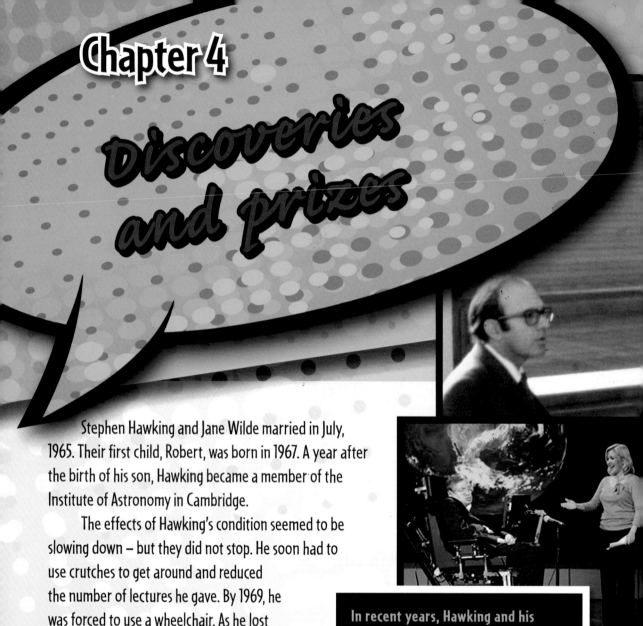

Stephen Hawking and Jane Wilde married in July, 1965. Their first child, Robert, was born in 1967. A year after the birth of his son, Hawking became a member of the Institute of Astronomy in Cambridge.

The effects of Hawking's condition seemed to be slowing down – but they did not stop. He soon had to use crutches to get around and reduced the number of lectures he gave. By 1969, he was forced to use a wheelchair. As he lost the ability to write things down, Hawking developed the remarkable talent of visualizing complex equations in his head.

In recent years, Hawking and his daughter, Lucy, have worked together to write a number of books for children.

Despite his physical setbacks, the next few years were exciting ones for Hawking. His daughter, Lucy, was born in 1970, and his research continued to bring attention. This was a hard time for Jane Hawking, though. She was struggling to complete her own PhD thesis at the same

Particle power

Hawking believes that, following a "big bang", many objects only the size of a proton (one of the building blocks of atoms) but with a mass of nearly a billion tonnes would be created, and these would then form mini black holes.

SUPERSTAR STAT

During the 1970s, Hawking and the US scientist Kip Thorne (third from left) debated theories about black holes.

time as looking after a young son, an increasingly disabled husband and now a new baby daughter. Life, however, was made much easier when, in 1971, Hawking won the annual international Gravity Research Foundation Award, with a piece on black holes.

Also in 1971, Hawking's investigations into the creation of the universe led him to predict that conditions at the beginning of a universe would be so extreme that matter would be forced into tiny superdense clumps forming, in effect, "mini" black holes. The unique feature of mini black holes is that while their immense mass and gravity mean that they are ruled by the laws of relativity, their minute size means that they are governed also by the laws of quantum mechanics.

Hawking then thought about how these mini black holes would interact with the space around them. In 1974, his calculations led him to a conclusion that at first he found so surprising he thought he must have made a mistake. Eventually, though, he came to believe he was right. A mini black hole would emit particles and eventually evaporate.

vanishing black holes

Hawking's findings about mini black holes were indeed surprising. Up until then it was thought that absolutely nothing got out of a black hole. Its powerfully concentrated gravity bent space and time to such a degree that nothing could escape from inside the event horizon. Hawking's calculations showed that a mini black hole would gradually lose mass and energy as particles escaped from it. How was this possible?

The answer is that the particles are not formed within the event horizon but just outside it. The laws of quantum mechanics allow the sharply curved space-time around the event horizon to cause tiny subatomic particles to form spontaneously. These particles form in pairs: one positive and one negative. Usually these particle pairs destroy each other in a fraction of a second. At the edge of a black hole event horizon, however, it is possible for one of the pairs to escape while the other falls back into the black hole. The particle

Hawking believes that black holes emit radiation and gradually disappear altogether.

Radical radiation

The idea of Hawking radiation and disappearing black holes was controversial at first. By the late 1970s, however, further research meant that Hawking's discovery came to be seen as a major breakthrough in physics.

STAR CONTRIBUTION

that enters the black hole has negative energy. It is the flow of negative energy particles into the black hole that causes it to lose mass and eventually to disappear in a sudden burst of radiation. This has become known as "Hawking radiation".

In March 1974, a few weeks after publishing his findings about black holes, Hawking became a Fellow of the Royal Society in London. At the age of 32 he was one of the youngest scientists to have been given this honour.

Hawking's success in showing that evaporating black holes could exist spurred him on to try to find a way to combine the theory of general relativity with quantum theory. His first book, *The Large Scale Structure of Space-Time*, published in 1973, continued his work on Einstein's theory of general relativity and the existence of singularities.

In 2009, US president Barack Obama presented Hawking with the Presidential Medal of Freedom.

Recognition of Hawking's achievements followed quickly. Growing public interest in the mysterious black holes led to him making several appearances on television to talk about his ideas.

In 1975, the Royal Astronomical Society in London awarded Hawking the Eddington Medal, for outstanding work in astrophysics. That same year he went to Rome, where he received the Pius XI medal for exceptional scientific promise from Pope Paul VI. More prizes came Hawking's way in 1976, including the Maxwell medal, awarded by the Institute of Physics in London for his work in theoretical physics, and the Hughes medal, given by the Royal Society for "distinguished contributions to the application of general relativity to astrophysics".

In autumn 1977, the University of Cambridge appointed Hawking to a professorship in gravitational physics. Rather than Doctor Hawking, he was now Professor Hawking. Then, two years later, came one of Hawking's greatest honours, when he was named Lucasian Professor of Mathematics at Cambridge, a

Maths master

Hawking became a professor of mathematics at Cambridge, one of the world's most prestigious universities, despite having received no formal maths instruction since leaving school in St. Albans at the age of 17.

When Hawking became Lucasian Professor at Cambridge he was following in the footsteps of the great scientist Isaac Newton.

distinguished position that had been held by just 16 other people, including Isaac Newton. His first lecture as Lucasian Professor was called "Is the End in Sight for Theoretical Physics?"

Also in 1979, Hawking received the very first Albert Einstein medal, given by the Albert Einstein Society in Switzerland for scientific work related to Einstein's theories. Back in the UK, in 1982, Hawking became a Commander of the British Empire (CBE), a rank just below that of a knight. He was also made a Companion of Honour, which is given in recognition of exceptional national service. There can be no more than 65 living members of the order at one time.

In 2009, Hawking was presented with the Presidential Medal of Freedom, the highest honour that can be given to a civilian in the United States. The one prize that continues to elude him, however, is the Nobel Prize for Physics.

Chapter 5

Trials and triumphs

Astronomers believe that an object in space called Cygnus-X1 is actually a star in orbit around a black hole.

At the same time as his research was taking him to the furthest reaches of the universe, Hawking's health was hampering him more and more, and putting increasing strain on his wife, Jane. When Hawking was appointed to a visiting professorship in 1975 at the California Institute of Technology (Caltech) in the United States, Jane suggested that one of Hawking's graduate students should come and live with them to help care for him. Hawking agreed with this, and so student Bernard Carr travelled to California with the Hawkings. He was the first of many students who took on the role of Hawking's helper.

While at Caltech, Hawking made a bet with a fellow scientist, the US physicist Kip Thorne, that a mysterious object in space called Cygnus X-1 was not, as Thorne thought, a star orbiting around an unseen black hole. The prize was a magazine subscription. Hawking said that if black holes did not exist he would have wasted a lot of work, but at least he would enjoy his magazine! Eventually, in 1990, he conceded that Thorne was probably right and settled the bet.

STAR CONTRIBUTION

Endless universe

In 1983, Hawking and US physicist Jim Hartle proposed the theory that the universe has no boundaries. They did this by combining ideas from quantum mechanics with general relativity. Hawking suggested comparing the universe to the surface of Earth. You can head off in any direction on Earth and never reach a point where it comes to an end. It is the same with the universe – except that Earth's surface is basically flat and two-dimensional, while the universe has four, or even more, dimensions.

By the late 1970s, Hawking could still feed himself and get out of bed, but needed help with most other things. His speech had become slurred, and close family and friends had to speak for him.

When they returned to Cambridge, Hawking and his wife argued with the university authorities about who should pay for the ramp he needed for his wheelchair. They also campaigned for better facilities and support at the university for students with disabilities.

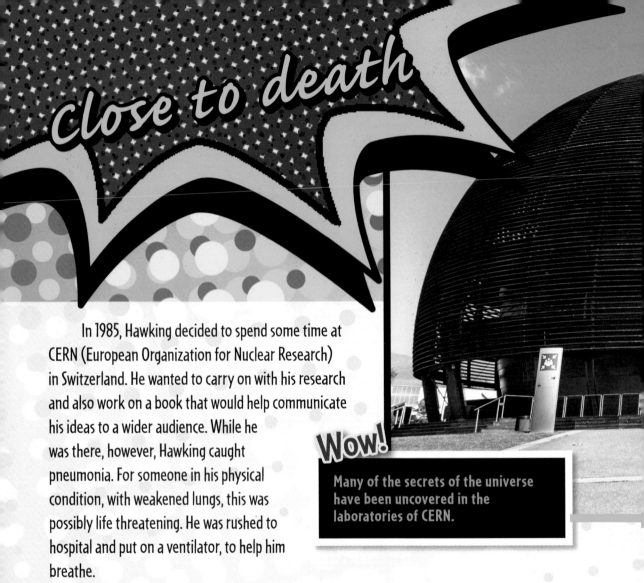

close to death

In 1985, Hawking decided to spend some time at CERN (European Organization for Nuclear Research) in Switzerland. He wanted to carry on with his research and also work on a book that would help communicate his ideas to a wider audience. While he was there, however, Hawking caught pneumonia. For someone in his physical condition, with weakened lungs, this was possibly life threatening. He was rushed to hospital and put on a ventilator, to help him breathe.

Wow!

Many of the secrets of the universe have been uncovered in the laboratories of CERN.

The doctors in the Swiss hospital thought Hawking was too far-gone to save and offered his wife, Jane, the option of turning off the ventilator machine to let him die. Jane refused and had him flown by air ambulance to Addenbrooke's Hospital, in Cambridge, where the doctors performed an emergency tracheostomy. This is a surgical procedure that involves cutting into the windpipe and inserting a tube that allows the person to breathe.

The operation was a success but it had meant cutting Hawking's vocal cords, making it impossible for him to speak. It also meant that he would now need round-the-clock care from a dedicated team of nurses for the rest of his life. Hawking has described the weeks of intensive care that followed the operation as being the darkest days of his life.

Beating the odds

Doctors are actually at a loss to explain how Hawking has survived so long with ALS. Most people who contract the condition are diagnosed after the age of 50 and expected to die within 5 years. Hawking was diagnosed at the age of 21 and is still alive in his 70s.

SUPERSTAR FACT

In early November 1985, Hawking returned home from Addenbroke's Hospital. His poor health was making it difficult for him to work and now he could not speak at all. The only way he could communicate with other people was to spell out words by raising his eyebrows when somebody pointed to the correct letter on a spelling card.

Now in his 70s, Hawking still makes many public appearances.

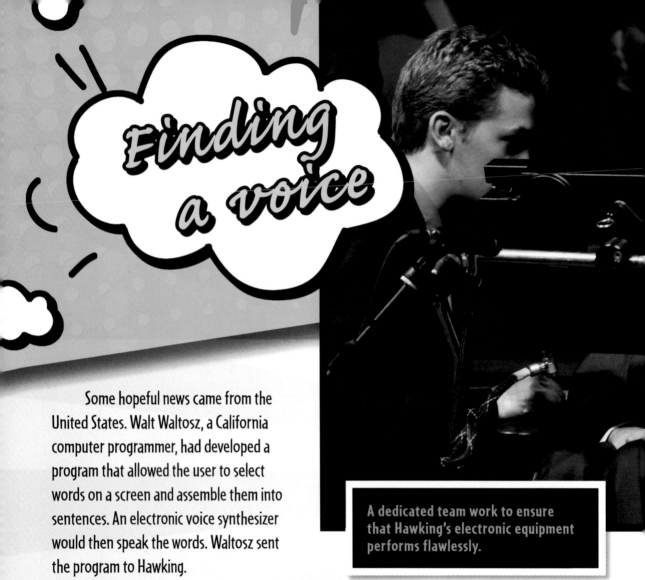

Finding a voice

A dedicated team work to ensure that Hawking's electronic equipment performs flawlessly.

Some hopeful news came from the United States. Walt Waltosz, a California computer programmer, had developed a program that allowed the user to select words on a screen and assemble them into sentences. An electronic voice synthesizer would then speak the words. Waltosz sent the program to Hawking.

The husband of one of Hawking's nurses was a computer engineer. He adapted a computer and synthesizer to Hawking's wheelchair so he could use the program. At first, Hawking selected his words with a handheld mouse. He now directs the program through a cheek muscle attached to a sensor. One small problem with the synthesizer was that it gave English Hawking an American accent, but he soon had fun opening his lectures with "Hello, please excuse my American accent."

If his computer was to stop working, Hawking would be cut off from the world. When he goes on a trip, there is far more to do than simply pack his passport and toothbrush. He travels with a large amount of backup hardware. Until recently, whenever Hawking went abroad, his assistants had

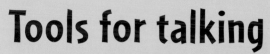

Tools for talking

The computer is just one piece of the total system Hawking depends on. This system includes not only the computer, but also the voice synthesizer, and a range of devices including a USB hub, audio amplifier and voice interface, power modules and the speaker through which his "voice" emerges.

SUPERSTAR FACT

Computer engineer Travis Bonifield holds a customized PC he designed specially for Hawking.

to dismantle the communication system from his main wheelchair, which he uses only in the UK, and mount the equipment onto a folding travel wheelchair.

Today, Hawking has a fully equipped travel chair, as well as his usual wheelchair. This has great advantages. If he has a new system installed he can easily be moved from one chair to the other while engineers carry out the work, and also his assistants no longer need to dismantle and install the system on a different chair every time he travels. They can simply switch Hawking's laptop from chair to chair, while he can be moved by his experienced helpers in just a few moments, free to carry on with his research.

Book breakthrough

Hawking feels strongly that as many people as possible should be able to read about his ideas.

In 1982, Hawking decided to write a book on cosmology that could be read by non-specialists. He wanted to write something that people would buy at airports and take on holiday with them. By 1984, he had produced a first draft of *A Brief History of Time*.

This was the book Hawking had been working on during his visit to CERN in Switzerland, when his life-threatening pneumonia prevented him from carrying on. When he was really ill, he despaired of ever finishing the book at all, but with the help of his new electronic voice he revised the work and it was published in spring 1988.

The launch party for the book's publication in the United States was held at the Rockefeller University in New York City. By all accounts, Hawking was full of energy and in a party mood, zipping around in his wheelchair from one guest to another. At one point, his wife, Jane, and his nurse were worried that he was getting so carried away he was going to wheel himself right into the East River!

Hawking the recordbreaker

By May 1995, *A Brief History of Time* had been in *The Sunday Times* bestseller list in the UK for 237 weeks, breaking the previous record of 184 weeks and winning Hawking a place in the 1998 *Guinness Book of Records*. Since its publication, the book has sold more than 10 million copies worldwide and been translated into more than 40 languages.

The first print run of 40,000 copies sold out almost immediately and the book was reprinted and rushed into bookshops. This was well before the days when people could simply download a book onto their e-reader. By the summer of 1988, *A Brief History of Time* had sold half a million copies in the United States alone, and been on the bestseller lists for four months.

In an interview, Hawking said that *A Brief History of Time* was the book he enjoyed writing most. A film version of the book, directed by Errol Morris and produced by Steven Spielberg, premiered in 1992.

Action!

Film director Steven Spielberg has been fascinated by space since he was a boy.

Chapter 6

A theory of everything

Many people were taken by surprise at how amazingly popular Hawking's books proved to be.

For a long time, Hawking has believed in the search for a "theory of everything", something that would unite quantum theory and relativity. *A Brief History of Time*, along with later books such as *The Universe in a Nutshell* and *The Grand Design*, illustrated Hawking's quest for an answer to science's great problem: a single unifying theory that can combine general relativity (governing the universe on a large scale) with quantum mechanics (the instruction book for the infinitely small).

Everything we know about the universe is based around four fundamental properties – space, time, mass and energy. Einstein's explanation for gravity is that it is a result of space-time being curved by the presence of mass and energy. In 1971, with his proposal for Hawking radiation, Hawking showed that sharply curved space-time could give rise to mass-energy (according to Einstein, mass and energy are just two different forms of the same thing).

Brain stretchers!

Hawking thinks that one way towards a theory of everything might lie in something called "M-theory". This mystifying theory involves such mindbenders as 11 dimensions of space-time, multiple universes, superstrings, supergravity and higher dimensional branes. Hawking explored these ideas in the book *The Grand Design*, written with US physicist Leonard Mlodinow in 2010.

SUPERSTAR FACT

Some of the amazing ideas Hawking explores can often seem like pure science fiction.

So, if mass-energy curves space-time and curved space-time causes mass-energy to appear, which came first? If they both appeared together simultaneously in the big bang, then what did they arise from? What in the universe could be more basic than space, time, mass and energy? No one knows the answer to the "which came first?" question, or even if the question itself is meaningful in any way that we could understand. "To understand the universe at the deepest level," Hawking says, "we have to understand why is there something rather than nothing. 'Why do we exist?'"

In the 1980s, Hawking declared that there was a 50 per cent chance that a theory unifying relativity and quantum mechanics would be found by 2000. Unfortunately, that has not happened.

Black hole bets

Professor Roger Penrose has worked with Hawking for more than 40 years.

The strain of dealing with her husband's increasing needs eventually became too much for Jane Hawking. In 1995, the couple divorced and Hawking remarried, this time to Elaine Mason, who was one of his nurses.

Through all of this, Hawking continued his researches and efforts to reach a wider audience for his ideas. He was still working with Roger Penrose, and in 1993 the two gave a series of lectures on "The Nature of Space and Time". Also in 1993, Hawking published a popular collection of essays and interviews called *Black Holes and Baby Universes and Other Essays*. This was followed by a six-part television series, *Stephen Hawking's Universe*, which appeared in 1997.

STAR CONTRIBUTION

Idea challenger

Hawking and other talented physicists may have plenty of fun making bets on these big questions, but it does not make them any less important. Hawking's idea that black holes could destroy information, challenged some of the most important ideas of quantum physics.

Wow!

A black hole's powerful gravity can bend light around it. At its centre is the mysterious event horizon.

In 1991, Hawking made a new black hole bet with Kip Thorne – and another Caltech physicist, John Preskill. Thorne and Preskill thought it was possible for a singularity to occur outside a black hole – a so-called "naked singularity". Hawking, backed up by Roger Penrose, said that this could not happen. In 1997, Hawking conceded the bet on what he called a "technicality", saying that naked singularities could form – but only under very special conditions.

Almost immediately afterwards, Preskilll made another bet with Hawking, this time concerning what happens to the information that is hidden behind a black hole's event horizon. Preskill bet that with the right kind of technology the information could be recovered from the radiation emitted as the black hole evaporated, while Hawking said the information would be destroyed. This time Thorne sided with Hawking. In 2004, Hawking outlined some new ideas he had about black holes that supported the conclusion that information loss does not occur after all. Again, he had to concede that Preskill might be right.

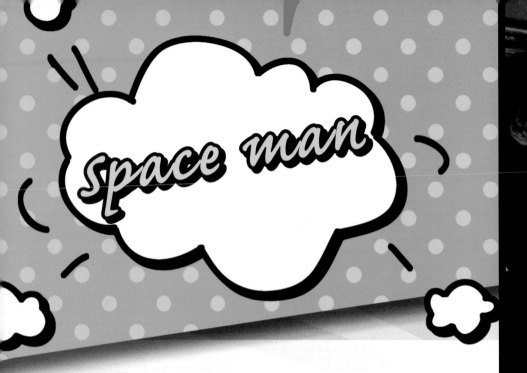

space man

In 2007, at the age of 65, Hawking visited the Kennedy Space Center in Florida, USA. There, he was given the chance to fly on a Boeing 727, which had been modified to give people, such as astronauts, training in weightlessness. During a two-hour flight over the Atlantic, the aeroplane made a series of rapid climbs and dives that allowed Hawking and the others on board to experience 25-second bursts of weightlessness. Fortunately, the interior of the plane was padded to avoid any injuries!

After the flight, Hawking said, "The zero-G [gravity] part was wonderful and the higher-G part was no problem. I could have gone on and on. Space, here I come!"

Hawking believes that private space vehicles

Hawking was absolutely thrilled by his experience of zero gravity aboard a modified aeroplane.

SUPERSTAR FACT

Funny physicist

An appearance on *The Simpsons* gave Hawking the chance to demonstrate his great sense of humour. When Principal Skinner tries to interpret for him, Hawking stops him with a sharp "Silence! I don't need anyone to talk for me – except this voicebox … ."

Hawking gave a series of lectures in praise of space travel to mark NASA's 50th anniversary in 2008.

will make space accessible to a greater number of people and he firmly intends to take his place on one of the first commercial flights into space. He has said that he does not believe the human race has a future unless it goes into space –in fact, he thinks the human race cannot survive another 1,000 years if it fails to make the leap into space. "Not to leave planet Earth would be like castaways on a desert island not trying to escape," he said. "Sending humans to other planets [...] will shape the future of the human race in ways we don't yet understand."

In the fictional world, Hawking has already been into space. In 1993, he appeared on the TV series *Star Trek: The Next Generation* as a hologram of himself playing poker with Commander Data, Albert Einstein and Isaac Newton. He has also appeared as himself on the sitcoms *The Simpsons* and *The Big Bang Theory*.

Look to the future

Hawking's health is a constant concern. In April 2009, a gravely sick Hawking, who had retired after 30 years as Lucasian Professor of Mathematics, was rushed to hospital but made a full recovery. He has reached his 70s with a disease that should have killed him by the age of 25. He says, "The doctor who diagnosed me with ALS told me it would kill me in two or three years. All my life, I have lived with the threat of an early death. So I hate wasting time."

In 2012, it was revealed that Hawking had taken part in trials for a new headband-style device called the iBrain, designed to pick up waves of electrical brain signals. He still works hard as a scientist, founding the Centre for Theoretical Cosmology (CTC) and acting as Director of Research at the Department of Applied Mathematics and Theoretical Physics (DAMTP), both at the University of Cambridge.

Science superstar!

Hawking's contributions to science have been immense. He has used Einstein's theory of general relativity to show how the universe began as a single point. He has investigated the properties of superdense black holes, even showing how they might evaporate and vanish in a burst of radiation. And he has shown how tiny variations in the conditions at the beginning of the universe have given rise to the stars and galaxies and made it possible for life, including us, to appear.

STAR CONTRIBUTION

Bang!

Hawking has fired the imaginations of many with his ideas about the workings of the universe.

Hawking continues to develop his theories about black holes and his hopes of being able to unite gravity with the forces at work in quantum mechanics. He even wonders if there really are such things as black holes. Instead of an event horizon, Hawking proposes an "apparent horizon", which instead of trapping matter and energy forever only imprisons them for a while, before eventually releasing them in a changed form. These are ideas that have developed over the 40 years since his first proposal of Hawking radiation.

Quantum theory, Hawking believes, "enables energy and information to escape from a black hole". Just how this process works will require a theory that successfully merges gravity with the other fundamental forces of nature that work on an atomic level – a goal that physicists, including Hawking, have struggled to achieve for nearly a century. As Hawking says, it "remains a mystery".

Glossary

astrophysics study of the physical make-up of planets, stars, galaxies and other objects in space

big bang rapid expansion of the universe from an infinitely small, infinitely dense point at the beginning of time

black hole region in space where matter has become so concentrated and the force of gravity so intense that nothing can escape from it, not even light

cosmology branch of science that studies the origin of the universe, how it has developed, and what might happen to it in the future

event horizon boundary line around a black hole that marks where the gravitational pull becomes strong enough to trap light. Nothing can be detected inside the event horizon.

galaxies systems of billions of stars. The galaxy our Sun belongs to is called the Milky Way.

general relativity theory put forward by the scientist Albert Einstein that explains that gravity is caused by the bending of space by the matter within it

gravitational fields space around an object where the effects of its gravity can be felt

gravity force of attraction that exists between objects – the more matter an object contains, the greater the pull of gravity it exerts

Hawking radiation radiation produced by a black hole due to particles being created just outside the event horizon

mass-energy mass (the amount of matter in something) representing a definite amount of energy

mini black holes black holes smaller than an atom, which would have to obey the laws of quantum mechanics. None have yet been proved to exist.

naked singularity singularity that is thought to exist outside a black hole event horizon

quantum mechanics branch of physics that deals with the behaviour of particles on the scale of atoms and even smaller

singularity point in which space is infinitely curved and matter infinitely dense

space-time idea, put forward by Albert Einstein, that space and time should be considered as a single four-dimensional property that is affected by mass and energy

steady-state theory theory (now abandoned) that proposed that new matter was constantly being created as the universe expanded

subatomic smaller than an atom

supernova star that suddenly increases greatly in brightness as a massive explosion throws most of its mass out into space

theoretical physics branch of physics that uses mathematics to explain how the universe works rather than carrying out experiments

universe all the matter and energy that exists and the space in which it exists

Find out more

Books

The Astronomy Book: Big Ideas Simply Explained, Robert Dinwiddie (DK Publishing, 2017)

George's Secret Key to the Universe, Lucy and Stephen Hawking (Corgi Childrens, 2008)

Space: A Children's Encyclopedia, DK (DK Reference, 2010)

Stephen Hawking (Against the Odds), Cath Senker (Raintree, 2015)

Websites

Watch videos that are full of facts about Stephen Hawking, at:
www.bbc.co.uk/science/space/universe/scientists/stephen_hawking

Find out more about Stephen Hawking, at:
www.dkfindout.com/uk/science/famous-scientists/stephen-hawking

Explore the story of the universe on the European Space Agency website, at:
www.esa.int/esaKIDSen/StoryoftheUniverse.html

Index

amyotrophic lateral sclerosis (ALS) 4, 15, 16, 33, 44
apparent horizon 45
astrophysics 14, 28
atoms 20, 22, 25

big bang 4, 19, 21, 25, 39
big bang theory 19
Big Bang Theory, The 43
black holes 4, 17, 20–21, 25, 26–27, 28, 30, 40–41, 45
Black Holes and Baby Universes and Other Essays 40
Brief History of Time, A 36–37, 38

Carr, Bernard 30
Centre for Theoretical Cosmology (CTC) 44
cosmology 14, 15, 18–23, 36
Cygnus X-1 30

Earth 31, 43
Eddington Medal 28
Einstein, Albert 4, 5, 11, 21, 22, 23, 27, 29, 38, 43, 45
energy 19, 20, 26, 27, 38, 39, 45
event horizon 21, 26, 41, 45

galaxies 18, 19, 23, 45
Galileo 6
Grand Design, The 38, 39
gravitational fields 23
gravitational physics 28
gravity 17, 20, 22, 23, 25, 26, 38, 42, 45
Gravity Research Foundation Award 25

Hartle, Jim 31
Hawking, Jane 16, 17, 24, 30, 32, 36, 40
Hawking radiation 27, 38, 45
Hoyle, Fred 14, 16
Hubble, Edwin 18
Hughes medal 28

iBrain 44
Institute of Astronomy 24
Institute of Physics 28

Kennedy Space Center 42

Large Scale Structure of Space-Time, The 27

mass 25, 26, 27, 38, 39
mass-energy 38–39
mathematics 11, 14, 16, 28, 29, 44
mini black holes 25, 26
Mlodinow, Leonard 39
motor neurone disease 4
M-theory 39

naked singularity 41
National Institute for Medical Research 9
Newton, Isaac 29, 43

particle physics 15
particles 15, 25, 26, 27
Penrose, Roger 17, 20, 21, 23, 40, 41
physics 4, 5, 8, 11, 12, 14, 15, 20, 21, 22, 27, 28, 29, 40, 44
Pius XI Medal 28
planets 18, 23, 43
Preskill, John 41
protons 25

quantum mechanics 4, 22–23, 25, 26, 31, 38, 39, 45
quantum physics 40

radiation 27, 38, 41, 45

Sciama, Dennis 14, 16, 17
singularity 20–21, 23, 41
space 4, 5, 18–21, 22, 25, 26–27, 30, 38, 42–43
space-time 38–39
stars 17, 18, 19, 20, 23, 30, 45
steady-state theory 14, 16, 19
Stephen Hawking's Universe 40
subatomic particles 15, 26
supernovas 20

telescopes 6, 18
theoretical physics 5, 8, 21, 28, 29
theory of everything 38–39
theory of general relativity 4, 14, 21, 22–23, 27, 28, 31, 38, 45
Thorne, Kip 30, 41
time 4, 21, 22, 26, 38, 39, 40

universe 4, 5, 14, 18–23, 25, 30, 31, 38–39, 45
Universe in a Nutshell, The 38

voice synthesizer 34, 35

Waltosz, Walt 34
weightlessness 42
Wheeler, John 20